EC-Council Associate C|CISO Certification Exam Prep

500 Practice Questions with Detailed Explanations

Introduction

The EC-Council Associate C|CISO Certification Exam Prep offers you a comprehensive guide to preparing for one of the most recognized certifications in the field of information security management. The Associate C|CISO certification is designed to validate your expertise in critical areas of cybersecurity leadership, making it a valuable credential for professionals aiming to step into senior roles in information security. With the growing need for cybersecurity experts, holding this certification signals your ability to manage security systems, ensure regulatory compliance, and mitigate risks at the organizational level.

This book contains 500 practice questions with detailed explanations that will sharpen your understanding of key topics. Some of the core areas covered include governance and risk management, information security controls, audit management, incident response, and legal compliance. By practicing these questions, you will not only prepare for the exam but also gain a deeper understanding of real-world scenarios that are crucial for success as a cybersecurity leader.

Earning the Associate C|CISO certification provides significant benefits, including increased credibility, enhanced career prospects, and a strong foundation in security program management. With this certification, you demonstrate your readiness to lead and secure modern enterprises, making you a valuable asset in any organization.

Practice Test Questions

Question 1

During an audit of a payment system for PCI-DSS compliance, an auditor needs to verify the protection of cardholder data. Which of the following encryption methods ensures data is unreadable to unauthorized users?

- A) Tokenization of cardholder data to replace sensitive elements with non-sensitive equivalents.
- B) Data masking of the full PAN whenever it is displayed.
- C) Data encryption using Advanced Encryption Standard (AES) with a 256-bit key length.
- D) Use of Secure Sockets Layer (SSL) certificates for secure data transmission.

Correct Answer: C

Explanation: AES with a 256-bit key length provides a high level of security that meets PCI-DSS standards for encryption, making it essential for the protection of cardholder data during storage and transmission.

Question 2

A company is revising its access control policy to ensure PCI-DSS compliance. Which practice is most effective for restricting access to cardholder data based on the need to know?

- A) Application of biometric authentication for system administrators only.
- B) Implementing role-based access control with stringent controls over privilege granting.
- C) Regular auditing of user access logs to detect any unauthorized access attempts.
- D) Enforcing a mandatory two-factor authentication for all users accessing sensitive information.

Correct Answer: B

Explanation: Role-based access control effectively minimizes access to sensitive cardholder data, ensuring that only personnel with legitimate business needs can access specific data sets, thus significantly reducing the risk of unauthorized data exposure.

Question 3

Fill in the blank: To maintain PCI-DSS compliance, it is essential that all system components and software are protected from known vulnerabilities by ensuring _____ are applied within one month of release.

- A) Security patches
- B) Antivirus software updates
- C) Continuous monitoring of network traffic
- D) Weekly vulnerability scans

Correct Answer: A

Explanation: Regular application of security patches is crucial for protecting against exploitation of known vulnerabilities, which can compromise cardholder data and violate PCI-DSS compliance.

Question 4

An e-commerce company uses multiple firewalls and DMZs to protect its cardholder data environment. Which of the following scenarios best illustrates compliance with PCI-DSS requirements for network security?

- A) Using a single firewall with stateful inspection to monitor incoming and outgoing traffic.
- B) Separate the network carrying cardholder data from the corporate network using a dual-firewall architecture.
- C) Utilizing network segmentation to limit access to the cardholder data environment.
- D) Installation of a single, robust firewall with intrusion detection capabilities.

Correct Answer: B

Explanation: Using a dual-firewall architecture to separate the network carrying cardholder data from other corporate networks provides an enhanced security layer, significantly decreasing the risk of external attacks and ensuring that access to sensitive data is controlled.

Question 5

A payment gateway processes transactions and suspects a data breach. As part of PCI-DSS compliance, what is the first step in the incident response plan?

- A) Immediate notification of all customers potentially affected by the breach.
- B) Conducting a thorough risk assessment to understand potential vulnerabilities in the system.
- C) Contacting the payment card brands to discuss the breach and potential fallout.
- D) Identifying and classifying the security incident to determine its severity and impact.

Correct Answer: D

Explanation: Identifying and classifying the incident promptly is critical in managing potential security breaches effectively. It allows the organization to implement specific responses based on the severity and impact of the incident, thus minimizing damage and maintaining compliance with PCI-DSS requirements.

Question 6

When assessing a healthcare application's compliance with HIPAA, what is essential to protect ePHI during transmission over unsecured networks?

- A) Conducting biannual penetration tests to identify vulnerabilities in the data

transmission process.
- B) Regularly updating firewall configurations to prevent unauthorized data access.
- C) Creating a secure channel for communication by using virtual private networks (VPNs).
- D) Implementing end-to-end encryption protocols such as SSL/TLS for all data transmissions.

Correct Answer: D

Explanation: End-to-end encryption such as SSL/TLS is essential for securing ePHI during transmission, as it ensures that the data remains unreadable and secure from unauthorized interception, adhering to HIPAA's requirement for safeguarding patient data during electronic exchanges.

Question 7

A healthcare provider is reviewing their HIPAA training program. What aspect should be emphasized to ensure compliance with the Privacy Rule?

- A) Regular updates on new healthcare legislation and how it impacts the management of ePHI.
- B) Ensuring all employees understand how to handle disclosures of ePHI with and without patient consent.
- C) Training on the technical aspects of ePHI storage solutions, focusing on data encryption.
- D) Incorporating scenarios and role-play exercises that simulate potential breaches of ePHI.

Correct Answer: B

Explanation: Understanding how to handle ePHI disclosures, particularly under scenarios requiring patient consent, is crucial for compliance with the HIPAA Privacy Rule, which mandates protection of personal health information and dictates the circumstances under which it can be disclosed.

Question 8

Fill in the blank: For HIPAA compliance, it is critical that every healthcare employee understands the minimum necessary standard when _____ ePHI.

- A) Archiving or retrieving
- B) Reviewing or auditing
- C) Accessing or sharing
- D) Storing or deleting

Correct Answer: C

Explanation: Knowledge of the minimum necessary standard is vital for HIPAA compliance, as it restricts access and sharing of ePHI to the least amount of information necessary to perform a task, thereby reducing the risk of unnecessary disclosure of sensitive information.

Question 9

In a scenario where a healthcare clinic must send ePHI to a billing company, what security measure ensures HIPAA compliance while maintaining data integrity?

- A) Implementing a biometric authentication system for all employees accessing the data remotely.
- B) Utilizing an encrypted VPN connection for all data transmissions between the clinic and the billing company.
- C) Requiring a two-factor authentication process for accessing any ePHI remotely.
- D) Applying digital signatures to each document containing ePHI before transmission.

Correct Answer: B

Explanation: Using an encrypted VPN for transmissions between a clinic and billing company ensures that ePHI remains secure and intact during transit, preventing data breaches and meeting HIPAA requirements for the safe transfer of sensitive information.

Question 10

After discovering unauthorized access to ePHI, what should a healthcare organization's first response include according to HIPAA regulations?

- A) Notifying the Department of Health and Human Services (HHS) within 24 hours.
- B) Conducting an immediate risk assessment to determine the breach's nature and scope.
- C) Immediate full data backup to secure the remaining ePHI from further unauthorized access.
- D) Alerting all patients potentially affected by the breach within the first week.

Correct Answer: B

Explanation: Performing a risk assessment immediately after detecting unauthorized access to ePHI helps to quickly evaluate the impact, scope of the breach, and identify compromised data, which is essential for effectively managing the situation and for subsequent notification procedures required by HIPAA.

Question 11

What is a mandatory requirement under SOX for ensuring the integrity of financial reporting data?

- A) Regular internal audits conducted by the company to ensure compliance with established controls.
- B) CEO and CFO certification of all financial reports before they are published.
- C) Annual third-party reviews of financial data to check for any discrepancies or fraud.
- D) Quarterly shareholder meetings to review financial performance and discuss any potential issues.

Correct Answer: A

Explanation: Regular internal audits are essential under SOX to verify that internal controls over financial reporting are effective and being adhered to, ensuring the accuracy and reliability of financial statements.

Question 12

Which method should be used to audit changes to financial software applications, in compliance with SOX regulations?

- A) Automated audit trails that capture all changes, approvals, and deployments.
- B) Use of checksums to verify that files have not been altered without proper authorization.
- C) Manual logs maintained by employees detailing all modifications to the applications.
- D) Peer reviews conducted by other developers within the company to ensure quality and security.

Correct Answer: A

Explanation: Automated audit trails provide a reliable and efficient method for tracking all changes made to financial software, facilitating transparency and accountability, which are core to SOX compliance.

Question 13

Fill in the blank: Under SOX, it is critical for companies to maintain _____ of all access to systems that affect financial reporting.

- A) Inspections
- B) Reports
- C) Verifications
- D) Logs

Correct Answer: D

Explanation: Maintaining logs of all access to systems related to financial reporting helps to ensure that any unauthorized or inappropriate access can be detected and addressed promptly, crucial for maintaining the integrity of financial data.

Question 14

In a scenario where a company's financial reporting software is updated, what is the best practice for compliance with SOX?

- A) Performing a comprehensive risk assessment prior to the update to identify potential security vulnerabilities.
- B) Skipping risk assessments to expedite the implementation of urgent updates.
- C) Immediate installation of updates to financial reporting software without prior testing.
- D) Consulting with external auditors to review the code changes before they are implemented.

Correct Answer: A

Explanation: Performing a risk assessment before implementing software updates is a best practice under SOX, as it ensures that any new risks introduced by the updates are identified and mitigated, maintaining the security and reliability of financial reporting systems.

Question 15

When setting up a new financial reporting system, what initial step must be taken to comply with SOX security requirements?

- A) Implement a strong access control system that limits access to financial data based on roles.
- B) Direct integration of financial reporting systems with public financial databases for enhanced transparency.

- C) Setting up a redundant data storage system to back up financial information periodically.
- D) Conducting a company-wide training on SOX compliance for all employees involved in the process.

Correct Answer: A

Explanation: Implementing strong access controls is a foundational step in securing financial systems under SOX, as it ensures that only authorized personnel have access to sensitive financial data, thereby protecting against unauthorized access and potential fraud.

Question 16

A federal agency is conducting a security review to ensure FISMA compliance. Which of the following steps is necessary for managing risk across all federal information systems?

- A) Implementing continuous risk assessments for all federal systems and networks.
- B) Establishing security training programs for all federal employees every quarter.
- C) Hiring external consultants to design security policies for each federal information system.
- D) Outsourcing security audits to third-party vendors to ensure compliance.

Correct Answer: A

Explanation: Continuous risk assessments ensure that federal agencies can identify and mitigate security vulnerabilities on an ongoing basis, a key requirement of FISMA to protect federal information systems.

Question 17

During the annual FISMA audit, a federal contractor discovers that one of their systems is non-compliant with the security controls. What is the most appropriate action to take for remediation under FISMA guidelines?

- A) Creating a Plan of Action and Milestones (POA&M) to address and correct the system vulnerabilities.
- B) Removing the system from operation until it can be brought into compliance.
- C) Disabling all non-compliant systems and reviewing the next audit cycle to address the gaps.
- D) Submitting a waiver request to delay compliance until the next fiscal year.

Correct Answer: A

Explanation: A Plan of Action and Milestones (POA&M) is required under FISMA to identify, track, and remediate security weaknesses, ensuring that vulnerabilities are addressed systematically and brought into compliance.

Question 18

Fill in the blank: FISMA requires all federal agencies to implement _____ to continuously monitor the effectiveness of their information security programs.

- A) Vulnerability scans
- B) Firewall configurations
- C) Continuous monitoring
- D) Patch management

Correct Answer: C

Explanation: Continuous monitoring of information security programs is critical for FISMA compliance, as it allows agencies to detect and respond to threats in real-time and maintain the integrity of federal information systems.

Question 19

A federal agency is planning to deploy a new cloud-based application. What process should the agency follow to ensure the application complies with FISMA regulations?

- A) Bypassing the risk assessment stage due to the system being hosted in a secure data center.
- B) Conducting a full risk assessment and submitting the system for an Authorization to Operate (ATO) review.
- C) Launching the application immediately, with a plan to update the security protocols post-deployment.
- D) Engaging third-party contractors to certify the security of the cloud-based application.

Correct Answer: B

Explanation: A full risk assessment followed by an Authorization to Operate (ATO) is mandatory for deploying any new systems under FISMA to ensure that the system meets all required security controls before being approved for operation.

Question 20

After a cyber incident affecting a federal information system, what should be the immediate next step to comply with FISMA's incident response requirements?

- A) Conducting a security patch and reporting the incident to internal audit departments.
- B) Reporting the incident to the federal authorities and conducting an immediate damage assessment.
- C) Isolating the compromised system and reconfiguring the firewall to prevent further attacks.
- D) Notifying all affected users and updating the agency's public incident log within 24 hours.

Correct Answer: B

Explanation: Immediate reporting of the incident to federal authorities and conducting a damage assessment is necessary for proper incident response under FISMA, ensuring that the breach is contained and evaluated to prevent future occurrences.

Question 21

A defense contractor is preparing for CMMC Level 3 certification. Which practice is crucial for ensuring that Controlled Unclassified Information (CUI) is properly protected during transmission?

- A) Creating a backup of all transmitted data in a secure offsite location.
- B) Setting up network segmentation to separate critical systems from less secure ones.
- C) Requiring users to digitally sign documents before transmitting them across networks.
- D) Using FIPS-validated encryption methods like AES-256 to secure data transmissions.

Correct Answer: D

Explanation: FIPS-validated encryption methods, such as AES-256, are essential for protecting data during transmission in compliance with CMMC regulations, ensuring that sensitive information is secure and unreadable by unauthorized parties.

Question 22

During a CMMC audit, the assessor reviews the contractor's system for managing access to sensitive DoD information. What security control must be in place to achieve compliance for CMMC Level 3?

- A) Role-based access controls applied strictly to administrators and key personnel.
- B) Multi-factor authentication for all users accessing Controlled Unclassified Information (CUI).
- C) Regularly rotating passwords every 30 days for all employees handling DoD contracts.
- D) Implementing a password policy requiring 12-character complex passwords across all systems.

Correct Answer: B

Explanation: Multi-factor authentication ensures that access to Controlled Unclassified Information (CUI) is only granted to authorized individuals by adding an additional layer of security beyond just a password, which is critical for achieving CMMC Level 3 compliance.

Question 23

Fill in the blank: To achieve CMMC Level 2 certification, companies must demonstrate _____ of all security incidents and provide documentation as evidence of their resolution.

- A) Vulnerability reports
- B) Incident logs
- C) Documentation
- D) Risk assessments

Correct Answer: C

Explanation: Proper documentation of security incidents and their resolution is crucial for demonstrating an organization's commitment to cybersecurity practices. CMMC Level 2 requires thorough record-keeping to provide evidence of compliance and effective incident management.

Question 24

A contractor is updating their cybersecurity policies to meet CMMC Level 5 requirements. What approach should the contractor take to ensure compliance while maintaining their operational effectiveness?

- A) Disabling all non-critical systems to reduce potential attack vectors during major updates.
- B) Implementing proactive threat hunting and continuous monitoring without disrupting daily operations.
- C) Engaging a third-party cybersecurity firm to handle all incident response efforts.
- D) Ensuring that updates to systems are applied immediately, regardless of business

impact.

Correct Answer: B

Explanation: Proactive threat hunting and continuous monitoring allow organizations to stay ahead of potential threats while maintaining operational effectiveness, which is a critical component of CMMC Level 5. This approach balances high-level security with day-to-day business needs.

Question 25

After detecting suspicious activity on their network, a defense contractor must comply with CMMC requirements for incident response. What is the first step the contractor should take to align with CMMC regulations?

- A) Running a full malware scan on all network devices and then performing forensics.
- B) Notifying all contractors and stakeholders of the potential breach within the first 24 hours.
- C) Isolating the affected network segment and initiating a full system shutdown.
- D) Reporting the activity to the Cybersecurity Maturity Model Certification (CMMC) accreditation body for further guidance.

Correct Answer: D

Explanation: Reporting suspicious activity to the CMMC accreditation body is the first step after detecting an incident, ensuring that proper procedures are followed for containment and mitigation while complying with CMMC incident response requirements.

Question 26

When processing personal data under GDPR, what is a necessary step to ensure lawful processing of data subject requests?

- A) Limiting the data processing to specific employees who have undergone GDPR training and certification.
- B) Implementing technical safeguards to protect data from accidental loss during processing.
- C) Storing the data securely in an encrypted format to protect it from unauthorized access.
- D) Obtaining explicit consent from the data subject prior to processing any personal information.

Correct Answer: D

Explanation: GDPR requires that data subjects provide explicit consent for the processing of their personal data. Without this consent, processing is unlawful, and organizations could face penalties for non-compliance.

Question 27

A company experiences a data breach exposing customer information. According to GDPR, what is the required action for the company within the first 72 hours of the breach?

- A) Immediately contacting law enforcement to conduct an investigation into the breach.
- B) Suspend all data processing activities until the breach has been fully mitigated and resolved.
- C) Notifying affected customers within 72 hours and providing them with guidance on how to protect their data.
- D) Reporting the breach to the relevant data protection authority along with all known details about the breach.

Correct Answer: D

Explanation: Under GDPR, organizations must notify the relevant data protection authority within 72 hours of becoming aware of a data breach. This is critical for ensuring transparency and swift action to mitigate any potential damage to affected individuals.

Question 28

Fill in the blank: GDPR mandates that organizations implement appropriate technical and organizational measures to ensure the confidentiality, integrity, and _____ of personal data.

- A) Backup
- B) Redundancy
- C) Availability
- D) Redaction

Correct Answer: C

Explanation: Availability is one of the core principles of GDPR. Organizations must ensure that personal data is not only kept confidential and secure but also remains available when needed, ensuring business continuity and compliance with GDPR.

Question 29

A multinational company is planning to transfer personal data from the EU to a non-EU country. What must the company do to ensure GDPR compliance during the data transfer?

- A) Execute a Standard Contractual Clause (SCC) with the receiving organization, outlining GDPR obligations.
- B) Ensure that the non-EU country offers an adequate level of protection as determined by the European Commission.
- C) Obtain a certification from a third-party auditor to verify that the receiving organization adheres to security standards.
- D) Implement data anonymization techniques before transferring the data outside the EU.

Correct Answer: B

Explanation: Transferring data outside of the EU requires that the receiving country provides an adequate level of protection, either through an adequacy decision by the European Commission or by using other legal mechanisms, such as Standard Contractual Clauses.

Question 30

After receiving a data erasure request under GDPR, what should an organization do to comply with the right to be forgotten?

- A) Retain the data for a minimum of five years to comply with internal policies before acting on the request.
- B) Anonymize the data and remove any references to the data subject without deleting the records.
- C) Notify the data subject that their data will be stored securely and provide them with a timeline for deletion.
- D) Erase all personal data relating to the data subject unless there is a legal obligation to retain it.

Correct Answer: D

Explanation: GDPR grants data subjects the right to request the erasure of their personal data. Organizations are obligated to delete this data unless there are legal grounds, such as regulatory or legal obligations, that require its retention.

Question 31

A business collects personal data from California residents. Under CCPA, what must the business include in its privacy notice to comply with data collection transparency requirements?

- A) Disclose the categories of personal data collected and the purposes for which the data will be used.
- B) Provide an option for consumers to download their collected data in a machine-readable format for portability purposes.
- C) Allow consumers to withdraw their consent for data collection at any time through an online portal.

- D) Ensure that personal data is encrypted and stored securely on their servers.

Correct Answer: A

Explanation: CCPA mandates that businesses collecting personal data from California residents must inform consumers about the categories of personal data collected and the specific purposes for which the data is used. This is crucial for maintaining transparency in data collection practices.

Question 32

After receiving a data deletion request from a California resident, what action must a business take to comply with CCPA regulations regarding the right to deletion?

- A) Move the data into a restricted database that limits employee access to authorized personnel only.
- B) Archive the data and restrict access, but retain it for business continuity purposes.
- C) Anonymize the data and keep it for research and development without using it for consumer-specific purposes.
- D) Permanently delete all personal information unless it is required to be retained for legal or business purposes.

Correct Answer: D

Explanation: Upon receiving a deletion request, CCPA requires businesses to delete the personal data of the consumer, unless there are legal or business reasons that necessitate its retention. This ensures compliance with consumers' right to request the deletion of their personal information.

Question 33

Fill in the blank: Under CCPA, businesses are required to provide consumers with a clear and easy-to-use method to _____ their personal data.

- A) Delete
- B) Opt-out of the sale of
- C) Encrypt
- D) Revoke

Correct Answer: B

Explanation: CCPA gives consumers the right to opt-out of the sale of their personal data to third parties. Businesses must provide a clear and easy method for consumers to exercise this right, protecting the consumer's control over their personal information.

Question 34

A company is using third-party services to manage customer data. What contractual agreement should the company establish to ensure compliance with CCPA when sharing consumer data?

- A) Include a clause in the agreement requiring the third-party provider to not use the data for any purposes other than those specified in the contract.
- B) Set up a technical service agreement that allows the third-party provider to manage data without any restrictions on use or storage.
- C) Implement a binding non-disclosure agreement (NDA) that prevents the third-party provider from sharing data with any external entities.
- D) Create a Memorandum of Understanding (MoU) outlining the data transfer process but without specific data usage limitations.

Correct Answer: A

Explanation: When sharing personal data with third-party providers, businesses must include specific clauses in contracts ensuring that the third party does not use the data for unauthorized purposes. This contractual obligation is key to maintaining CCPA compliance when transferring or processing consumer data.

Question 35

A California resident requests information on how their personal data is being used by a company. What must the company do to comply with the CCPA within 45 days of the request?

- A) Provide a detailed report outlining the types of data collected, how it is used, and the third parties with whom it is shared.
- B) Conduct an internal audit and issue a summary report that highlights data security protocols without revealing detailed data usage information.
- C) Issue a public statement explaining the company's data collection policies and offering general information about data sharing practices.
- D) Respond with a summary of the company's data security measures, but avoid disclosing specific details on data usage or sharing.

Correct Answer: A

Explanation: The CCPA requires businesses to respond to a consumer's request for information within 45 days by providing a comprehensive report that details the types of personal data collected, how it is used, and with whom it is shared. This empowers consumers to understand and control how their personal information is being handled.

Question 36

When implementing ISO 27001 for certification, what step is necessary to establish an effective information security management system (ISMS)?

- A) Purchase cybersecurity insurance to cover potential risks associated with data breaches.
- B) Conduct a comprehensive risk assessment to identify threats, vulnerabilities, and impacts on information assets.
- C) Deploy intrusion detection systems (IDS) to monitor and detect unauthorized access to critical systems.

- D) Implement strong encryption protocols for all sensitive data stored on company servers.

Correct Answer: B

Explanation: A comprehensive risk assessment is fundamental to implementing an effective ISMS under ISO 27001. This process identifies potential security risks to information assets, which is critical for applying appropriate controls to mitigate those risks.

Question 37

A company is preparing for its ISO 27001 audit and must ensure compliance with the standard's risk assessment requirements. What is the most appropriate method to manage identified risks under ISO 27001?

- A) Develop and maintain a risk treatment plan that addresses the identified risks and includes assigned responsibilities.
- B) Ignore minor risks and only address high-impact risks to avoid unnecessary resource allocation.
- C) Perform vulnerability scans regularly but avoid addressing the risks until the next audit cycle.
- D) Distribute responsibility for risk mitigation to individual departments without a formal plan.

Correct Answer: A

Explanation: A risk treatment plan is required under ISO 27001 to manage identified risks. It outlines how each risk will be treated, assigns responsibilities, and ensures that controls are in place to minimize threats to the organization's information security.

Question 38

Fill in the blank: ISO 27001 requires organizations to implement _____ to continuously monitor and improve their information security controls.

- A) Employee awareness programs
- B) Incident response teams
- C) Patch management schedules
- D) Continual improvement processes

Correct Answer: D

Explanation: ISO 27001 promotes continual improvement processes to ensure that security controls evolve over time and remain effective in addressing emerging threats and vulnerabilities. This process ensures ongoing compliance and adaptation to changes.

Question 39

A multinational corporation is undergoing ISO 27001 certification and needs to demonstrate effective control over third-party vendors. What process should the company follow to comply with vendor management requirements under ISO 27001?

- A) Establish formal agreements with vendors that outline information security requirements and audit rights.
- B) Train internal staff on vendor management procedures without requiring external audits.
- C) Require vendors to follow internal security policies without formalizing any contractual agreements.
- D) Use a third-party contractor to manage vendor relationships but avoid granting them access to sensitive data.

Correct Answer: A

Explanation: Managing third-party vendors under ISO 27001 requires formal agreements that define security expectations and grant the company rights to audit vendor compliance. This ensures vendors do not pose a security risk to the organization.

Question 40

During an internal audit of the ISMS, a critical security incident occurs involving unauthorized access to sensitive information. What should the organization do to maintain ISO 27001 compliance in response to the incident?

- A) Perform a full system rollback to a previous version and delay any further actions until instructed by management.
- B) Shut down the affected systems and wait for the external audit to occur before documenting the incident.
- C) Document the incident, conduct a thorough investigation, and implement corrective actions based on the findings.
- D) Implement temporary access restrictions but avoid involving external auditors until the audit is due.

Correct Answer: C

Explanation: Incident documentation and investigation are essential components of ISO 27001. By documenting the incident, investigating the root cause, and implementing corrective actions, the organization ensures that similar incidents do not recur, maintaining the integrity of the ISMS.

Question 41

A cybersecurity analyst is tasked with integrating the NIST Cybersecurity Framework into an organization's existing security policies. The analyst's first step is to assess how current security practices align with which NIST function?

- A) Detect
- B) Respond
- C) Identify
- D) Protect

Correct Answer: C

Explanation: The Identify function is crucial as it helps organizations understand their environment and systems which is fundamental before aligning practices with the NIST framework.

Question 42

While conducting a gap analysis for a company, a consultant notices several areas where the company's incident response does not meet NIST standards. Which NIST function primarily focuses on mitigating the impact of cybersecurity events?

- A) Respond
- B) Govern
- C) Recover
- D) Identify

Correct Answer: A

Explanation: The Respond function deals with developing and implementing actions to mitigate the effects of cybersecurity incidents which aligns with the consultant's focus in the scenario.

Question 43

What is the primary component of the NIST Cybersecurity Framework that directly supports proactive risk management by emphasizing the least privilege and access control measures?

- A) Protect
- B) Identify
- C) Recover
- D) Detect

Correct Answer: A

Explanation: The Protect function includes safeguards like access control policies that enforce the principle of least privilege, essential for proactive risk management.

Question 44

In the context of the NIST Cybersecurity Framework, which function would be most concerned with the establishment and improvement of systems designed to detect cybersecurity events?

- A) Govern
- B) Protect
- C) Detect
- D) Respond

Correct Answer: C

Explanation: The Detect function is critical for the timely discovery of cybersecurity events which helps organizations in reacting and adapting to threats swiftly.

Question 45

Fill in the blank: The _____ function of the NIST Cybersecurity Framework focuses on the recovery plans and backups to maintain resilience and restore capabilities after a cybersecurity incident.

- A) Recovery
- B) Protect
- C) Identify
- D) Respond

Correct Answer: A

Explanation: The Recovery function is designed to help organizations restore impaired services and repair systems following an incident, emphasizing the importance of resilience and robust recovery strategies.

Question 46

Which SOC 2 trust service criterion ensures that the system is protected against unauthorized access both physically and logically?

- A) Availability
- B) Processing Integrity
- C) Security
- D) Confidentiality

Correct Answer: C

Explanation: The Security criterion is pivotal as it encompasses the measures that protect against unauthorized access, ensuring the system remains protected both physically and logically.

Question 47

A company uses cloud storage for client data. Which SOC 2 trust service criterion most directly addresses the availability and functionality of this system for operation and use as committed?

- A) Processing Integrity
- B) Availability
- C) Confidentiality

- D) Security

Correct Answer: B

Explanation: The Availability criterion ensures that the services are available for operation as committed, which is crucial for clients relying on continuous access to cloud storage.

Question 48

Fill in the blank: The SOC 2 criterion that focuses on the completeness, validity, accuracy, and timeliness of the system's outputs is called _____.

- A) Processing Integrity
- B) Security
- C) Confidentiality
- D) Availability

Correct Answer: A

Explanation: Processing Integrity ensures that data processing is complete, valid, accurate, and timely, thus maintaining the integrity and reliability of the system's outputs.

Question 49

In a review of an organization's compliance with SOC 2, the auditor is examining the encryption and disposal procedures of data. Which trust service criterion are they primarily assessing?

- A) Availability
- B) Integrity
- C) Confidentiality
- D) Security

Correct Answer: C

Explanation: The Confidentiality criterion is focused on protecting information designated as confidential, through encryption and proper disposal, to maintain its secrecy.

Question 50

An IT firm is preparing for a SOC 2 Type II report. Which criterion would require the firm to demonstrate the operation of controls over a defined period?

- A) Security
- B) Confidentiality
- C) Processing Integrity
- D) Availability

Correct Answer: C

Explanation: For a SOC 2 Type II report, demonstrating the effectiveness of operational controls over a defined period is essential under the Processing Integrity criterion to ensure consistent performance in data processing.

Question 51

In the context of cyber resilience, what step should a company take first when developing a strategy to mitigate the impact of a cyber-attack on its operational capabilities?

- A) Reviewing and updating all existing security policies and protocols.
- B) Conducting a comprehensive risk assessment to identify critical assets and vulnerabilities.
- C) Training employees on basic cybersecurity awareness and hygiene practices.
- D) Purchasing cyber insurance to cover potential financial losses.

Correct Answer: B

Explanation: Conducting a comprehensive risk assessment as a first step allows the organization to identify and prioritize critical assets and vulnerabilities, ensuring that resources are allocated effectively to areas of greatest need, which is essential in developing a focused and effective cyber resilience strategy.

Question 52

A cybersecurity manager is analyzing threats to develop cyber resilience. What is the most critical element they should consider to enhance the system's ability to recover quickly?

- A) The type of malware most commonly detected in company systems.
- B) The estimated financial impact of potential threats on company assets.
- C) The time it takes for systems to revert to operational status after an incident.
- D) The geographical locations of the company's data centers and operations.

Correct Answer: C

Explanation: Focusing on the recovery time of systems ensures that the organization plans adequately for fast recovery, which is crucial in maintaining operational continuity and reducing downtime, thereby enhancing overall cyber resilience.

Question 53

Fill in the blank: In the field of cyber resilience, _____ refers to the ability of a system to continue operating despite the occurrence of a cyber-attack.

- A) resilience
- B) flexibility
- C) redundancy

- D) adaptability

Correct Answer: C

Explanation: Redundancy is crucial in cyber resilience as it ensures that there are additional systems or modules that can take over functions if primary systems fail, allowing operations to continue without significant interruptions.

Question 54

Which of the following strategies is best for a company that wants to ensure continuity of operations during a ransomware attack?

- A) Hiring a third-party cybersecurity firm to handle incident responses.
- B) Mandating multi-factor authentication for all system access points.
- C) Implementing an automated data backup system in multiple geographically diverse locations.
- D) Isolating critical network segments from each other to prevent spread.

Correct Answer: C

Explanation: An automated data backup system that stores data in multiple, geographically diverse locations ensures that if one location is compromised by a ransomware attack, other locations remain unaffected, enabling quick restoration of data and continuity of operations.

Question 55

When designing a cyber resilience strategy, which method is considered effective in protecting data integrity during a breach?

- A) Conducting frequent, unannounced penetration testing to identify vulnerabilities.
- B) Utilizing encryption to safeguard data both at rest and in transit.

- C) Establishing a dedicated incident response team that is trained regularly.
- D) Regularly updating and patching all software and systems used by the company.

Correct Answer: B

Explanation: Encryption is vital for protecting data integrity during a breach as it makes data unreadable without the correct decryption key, ensuring that sensitive information remains secure and private even if unauthorized access is gained.

Question 56

When implementing data classification policies in a corporation, what is the primary role of data owners?

- A) Creating detailed documentation on the procedures involved in data handling.
- B) Monitoring and logging access and usage of data to ensure compliance.
- C) Defining the sensitivity levels of the data they oversee and approving classification.
- D) Installing technical controls to prevent unauthorized data access.

Correct Answer: C

Explanation: Data owners play a crucial role in defining the sensitivity of the data under their control, as they are most familiar with the data's characteristics and the impact of its potential exposure. Their approval of classification levels is essential to ensure that data is handled appropriately throughout its lifecycle.

Question 57

An organization is revising its data classification policy. Which criterion is most important for defining the levels of data classification?

- A) The amount of data the organization stores and processes.

- B) The ease of data replication and distribution across multiple platforms.
- C) The potential impact of data exposure or breach on the organization.
- D) The age of the data being stored, particularly for compliance with legal requirements.

Correct Answer: C

Explanation: The potential impact of data exposure or breach on the organization dictates the level of protection required. Classifying data based on this criterion ensures that the most sensitive data receives the highest level of security, which is critical for protecting the organization's interests and maintaining compliance with regulatory requirements.

Question 58

Fill in the blank: Effective data classification policies categorize data based on its _____ to determine the necessary level of security.

- A) complexity
- B) sensitivity
- C) volume
- D) utility

Correct Answer: B

Explanation: Sensitivity is a fundamental criterion for data classification as it directly relates to the risks associated with unauthorized access or data breaches. Classifying data based on sensitivity ensures that security measures are proportionate to the potential risks, thereby optimizing resource allocation and enhancing data protection strategies.

Question 59

In an enterprise setting, what is a critical first step in implementing a data classification policy?

- A) Conducting employee training sessions on the importance and methods of data classification.
- B) Updating all privacy policies to reflect new data classification standards.
- C) Identifying and categorizing all data assets within the organization based on sensitivity.
- D) Deploying encryption technologies across all organizational data.

Correct Answer: C

Explanation: Identifying and categorizing all data assets based on their sensitivity is a critical first step in implementing a data classification policy. This initial categorization forms the foundation for all subsequent security measures and policies, ensuring that data is protected according to its value and vulnerability.

Question 60

During a data classification audit, which practice is essential to ensure the classification remains accurate and compliant?

- A) Periodically testing data security measures to check for potential vulnerabilities.
- B) Regularly reviewing and updating the classification rules and the data classified under them.
- C) Implementing a technology solution that automatically classifies data based on content.
- D) Training all new employees on the importance of data classification policies.

Correct Answer: B

Explanation: Regular reviews and updates of classification rules and the data under them are essential for maintaining the accuracy and relevance of data classification systems. As organizational needs change and new threats emerge, updating classification ensures compliance and continued protection of sensitive information.

Question 61

What is the most critical factor in reducing detection time of security incidents within a network?

- A) Frequent training sessions for IT staff on new cyber threats.
- B) Integration of automated threat detection systems with real-time alerts.
- C) Periodic review and testing of network security measures.
- D) Regular updating of antivirus signatures and firewall rules.

Correct Answer: B

Explanation: The integration of automated threat detection systems with real-time alerts is critical for reducing detection time because it enables organizations to quickly identify and respond to threats before they can escalate, thereby minimizing potential damage and improving overall security posture.

Question 62

A cybersecurity team is conducting a post-incident review. What is the primary focus of this analysis to enhance future response efforts?

- A) Identifying any delays or failures in the existing response processes.
- B) Determining the root cause of the security breach.
- C) Reviewing the communication effectiveness between departments.
- D) Assessing the financial impact of the incident on the organization.

Correct Answer: A

Explanation: Identifying delays or failures in the response processes during a post-incident review is crucial because it helps pinpoint weaknesses in the incident response strategy. Understanding where the process faltered allows for targeted improvements to be made, enhancing the speed and effectiveness of future responses.

Question 63

Fill in the blank: In incident response, the initial _____ phase is crucial for understanding the scope and impact of an incident.

- A) identification
- B) containment
- C) recovery
- D) eradication

Correct Answer: A

Explanation: The identification phase in incident response is fundamental because it involves determining the nature and extent of an incident. Quick and accurate identification is essential to formulating an effective response, as it sets the stage for containment and eradication efforts, directly impacting the resolution of the incident.

Question 64

During a simulated attack, a response team failed to contain a breach effectively. What should be the first action in the debriefing session?

- A) Updating the security protocols and access controls immediately.
- B) Focusing on improving the technical skills of the response team.
- C) Reviewing the timeline and methods used to detect and respond to the breach.
- D) Analyzing the impact of the breach on customer data privacy.

Correct Answer: C

Explanation: Reviewing the timeline and methods used in the detection and response phases during a debriefing session is essential to understand where the process may have failed and how it can be improved. This review helps identify missed opportunities for quicker detection and more effective containment, which are critical for refining response strategies.

Question 65

An organization discovered unauthorized access to its systems. What should be the initial step in the incident response?

- A) Notifying all users about the breach and advising on necessary precautions.
- B) Running a full system scan to identify all affected files and programs.
- C) Isolating the affected systems to prevent further unauthorized access.
- D) Consulting with external cybersecurity experts to analyze the breach.

Correct Answer: C

Explanation: Isolating the affected systems is the most immediate and effective step to take following the discovery of unauthorized access. This action prevents further damage by stopping the spread of the breach to other areas of the network, securing potentially unaffected data and systems while the incident is further investigated and resolved.

Question 66

In the event of a detected security breach, what is the most effective initial action for an incident response team?

- A) Immediate isolation of the affected systems to contain the breach.
- B) Running antivirus scans on all workstations connected to the network.
- C) Alerting all employees about the breach via email to ensure they are aware.
- D) Directing IT staff to back up critical data immediately.

Correct Answer: A

Explanation: Isolating affected systems immediately helps to prevent the spread of the breach and limits potential damage, allowing the incident response team to manage and mitigate the impact in a controlled and secure manner.

Question 67

An incident responder finds evidence of an advanced persistent threat (APT) in the network. What should their first technical response be?

- A) Increasing the logging level of all systems to gather more detailed information.
- B) Disabling internet access to prevent external communications.
- C) Applying network segmentation to limit further lateral movement of the APT.
- D) Shutting down all system operations to prevent data loss.

Correct Answer: C

Explanation: Applying network segmentation as soon as an APT is detected effectively restricts the threat's capability to move laterally across the network, which is critical in limiting the reach and impact of the attacker within compromised environments.

Question 68

Fill in the blank: An essential component of incident response is the establishment of a _____ to coordinate the response actions efficiently.

- A) rapid response team
- B) threat analysis team
- C) command center
- D) impact assessment group

Correct Answer: C

Explanation: Establishing a command center is crucial in incident response as it serves as a central point for coordination and communication. This setup ensures that all response actions are streamlined and that information flows efficiently among all stakeholders involved in managing the incident.

Question 69

A company experiences a sudden network outage suspected to be a denial-of-service attack. What should the first investigative step be?

- A) Checking the integrity and capacity of network security devices like firewalls and routers.
- B) Contacting external cybersecurity firms for immediate intervention.
- C) Releasing an official statement to the public about the incident.
- D) Resetting all user passwords to cut off unauthorized access.

Correct Answer: A

Explanation: Checking network security devices for integrity and capacity immediately after a suspected denial-of-service attack is essential. It helps determine if these devices were compromised or overwhelmed, which is crucial for both mitigating the attack and planning recovery actions.

Question 70

When conducting a forensic analysis post-incident, what is crucial to maintaining the integrity of the data?

- A) Interviewing staff to determine any unusual activities or access patterns.
- B) Deploying additional security patches across vulnerable systems.
- C) Reviewing access logs to determine who was logged in at the time of the incident.
- D) Creating a bitwise image of affected systems before performing any further analysis.

Correct Answer: D

Explanation: Creating a bitwise image of affected systems is fundamental in forensic analysis to ensure that all digital evidence is preserved in its original state. This process allows for accurate analysis without altering the data, which is critical for any subsequent legal actions or detailed investigations.

Question 71

What is the primary goal of having an off-site backup location in disaster recovery planning?

- A) Facilitating regulatory compliance by having multiple data storage locations.
- B) Ensuring data availability and business continuity even after catastrophic events.
- C) Allowing IT staff to operate remotely in the event of a local network failure.
- D) Reducing the cost of data storage by utilizing geographically distant data centers.

Correct Answer: B

Explanation: The primary goal of maintaining an off-site backup location in disaster recovery planning is to ensure data availability and business continuity. By storing backups in a geographically separate location, organizations protect critical data from being lost or inaccessible in the event of a disaster at the primary site, thereby supporting continuous operational capability.

Question 72

When reviewing a disaster recovery plan, what is the most crucial element to evaluate for ensuring data recovery within an acceptable timeframe?

- A) Testing the backup generators and UPS systems in the primary data center.
- B) The frequency of backup generation for archived data.
- C) The Recovery Time Objective (RTO) for critical systems.
- D) Regularly updating the contact information for all disaster recovery team members.

Correct Answer: C

Explanation: The Recovery Time Objective (RTO) is crucial in disaster recovery planning as it defines the maximum acceptable length of time that a system's functionality can be unavailable after a disaster without causing significant harm to the business. Evaluating and setting appropriate RTOs for critical systems ensures that recovery efforts focus on restoring the most important operations first to minimize downtime and impact.

Question 73

Fill in the blank: Effective disaster recovery plans typically include detailed _____ procedures to ensure rapid restoration of IT systems.

- A) failover
- B) backup
- C) documentation
- D) recovery

Correct Answer: A

Explanation: Including detailed failover procedures in a disaster recovery plan is essential for ensuring the rapid restoration of IT systems. Failover procedures outline how systems transition to a secondary operational status when the primary setup fails, thereby maintaining service continuity crucial for business operations during a crisis.

Question 74

After a major data center disaster, what should be the first action according to a well-structured disaster recovery plan?

- A) Activating the disaster recovery site and redirecting network traffic.
- B) Conducting an immediate review of disaster recovery protocols to identify failures.
- C) Informing all employees about the disaster through the internal communication system.
- D) Assessing the financial impact of the disaster to prepare a report for stakeholders.

Correct Answer: A

Explanation: Activating the disaster recovery site and redirecting network traffic is the first action that should be taken following a major data center disaster according to a well-structured disaster recovery plan. This step is critical to quickly restoring system availability and access to data, thus minimizing downtime and maintaining business operations.

Question 75

In the planning of disaster recovery strategies, what is critical for ensuring the organization can operate during a major IT system failure?

- A) Updating all software applications to the latest versions to avoid vulnerabilities.
- B) Establishing an alternate processing site to handle critical operations.
- C) Conducting regular audits on the physical security of the primary data center.
- D) Purchasing insurance to cover potential losses from IT system downtimes.

Correct Answer: B

Explanation: Establishing an alternate processing site for handling critical operations is fundamental in disaster recovery strategies to ensure that the organization can continue operating during major IT system failures. Alternate sites allow businesses to maintain critical functions without interruption, which is essential for the continuity of operations and minimizing financial and operational impacts.

Question 76

What is the key objective of Business Continuity Planning (BCP) for IT systems in a multinational corporation?

- A) Ensuring that critical business operations can continue with minimal downtime.
- B) Reducing insurance premiums by demonstrating risk mitigation strategies.
- C) Focusing on protecting company data from potential cyber threats only.
- D) Increasing the resilience of IT infrastructure by adopting new technologies.

Correct Answer: A

Explanation: The primary goal of Business Continuity Planning (BCP) for IT systems, especially in a multinational corporation, is to ensure that critical business operations can continue with minimal downtime. This ensures that the company can maintain essential services and functions during a disruption, which is crucial for sustaining operational effectiveness and maintaining customer trust and regulatory compliance.

Question 77

When conducting a business impact analysis for BCP, what is the primary focus?

- A) Identifying critical business functions and the impact of their disruption.
- B) Estimating the time required to recover different business functions.
- C) Calculating the financial return on investment for continuity measures.
- D) Assessing the physical security measures at all business locations.

Correct Answer: A

Explanation: In conducting a business impact analysis for BCP, the primary focus is on identifying critical business functions and understanding the impact of their disruption. This analysis helps to prioritize resources and recovery strategies, ensuring that the most crucial areas of the business receive immediate attention during and after an incident, minimizing both downtime and financial losses.

Question 78

Fill in the blank: Business Continuity Planning must prioritize maintaining _____ operations during a disruption.

- A) all
- B) critical
- C) financial
- D) remote

Correct Answer: B

Explanation: Maintaining critical operations during a disruption is a core priority of Business Continuity Planning. Ensuring that these essential functions can continue uninterrupted or be resumed quickly is essential for the survival of the company during crises, supporting both operational sustainability and strategic resilience.

Question 79

A financial institution is updating its BCP in light of new regulatory requirements. What is the first action they should take?

- A) Conducting a full-scale drill to test the response to hypothetical scenarios.
- B) Training staff on new evacuation procedures in case of emergencies.
- C) Reviewing current BCP compliance with the latest regulatory standards.
- D) Revising the company's insurance coverage to include disaster recovery.

Correct Answer: C

Explanation: Reviewing current BCP compliance with the latest regulatory standards is the first action that should be taken when updating a business continuity plan, especially for a financial institution affected by regulatory requirements. This ensures that all aspects of the plan are up to date and meet all legal obligations, which is critical for legal compliance and operational readiness.

Question 80

During a regional power outage, what is the first step a company should take according to their BCP?

- A) Assessing the financial impact of the outage on quarterly earnings.
- B) Switching to an alternative power supply to maintain operational continuity.
- C) Immediately informing customers and partners about potential service delays.
- D) Sending all employees home until the power is fully restored.

Correct Answer: B

Explanation: Switching to an alternative power supply as a first response during a regional power outage is crucial for maintaining operational continuity. This step ensures that critical systems and operations can continue functioning, which is vital for minimizing disruptions to services and maintaining business functions during external power failures.

Question 81

What is the primary purpose of penetration testing in a corporate security environment?

- A) Ensuring compliance with international standards for cybersecurity.
- B) Evaluating the effectiveness of training programs for new security personnel.
- C) Identifying vulnerabilities in systems and networks before attackers can exploit them.
- D) Testing the response time of the IT support team in case of security incidents.

Correct Answer: C

Explanation: Penetration testing serves as a proactive measure to identify vulnerabilities in systems and networks that could be exploited by attackers. By simulating an attack under controlled conditions, organizations can understand potential weaknesses and rectify them before they are exploited in a real-world scenario, thereby strengthening their security posture.

Question 82

Which method is most effective for assessing the physical security of a data center as part of a comprehensive security audit?

- A) Installing additional surveillance cameras and motion detectors around the perimeter.
- B) Using drones to monitor the external perimeter of the facility continuously.
- C) Conducting a controlled physical breach attempt with a simulated intruder.
- D) Reviewing video surveillance footage for any signs of past unauthorized access.

Correct Answer: C

Explanation: Conducting a controlled physical breach attempt with a simulated intruder is an effective method for assessing physical security measures at a data center. This approach tests the actual efficacy of security protocols and physical barriers, providing realistic insights into the security team's response capabilities and the potential for unauthorized access.

Question 83

Fill in the blank: Continuous _____ monitoring is crucial for validating security measures and identifying potential breaches.

- A) threat
- B) vulnerability
- C) network
- D) performance

Correct Answer: B

Explanation: Continuous vulnerability monitoring is essential in a security environment as it helps to consistently validate the effectiveness of implemented security measures and quickly identify and address new vulnerabilities or threats. This proactive surveillance allows organizations to maintain high security standards and react swiftly to potential breaches.

Question 84

In preparing for a security audit, what critical step should be taken first to ensure the scope of the audit is comprehensive?

- A) Updating the company's cybersecurity insurance policy coverage.
- B) Reviewing all current security policies and infrastructure documentation.
- C) Interviewing IT staff about their awareness and implementation of security practices.
- D) Checking for software updates and patch levels on critical systems.

Correct Answer: B

Explanation: Reviewing all current security policies and infrastructure documentation is a critical first step in preparing for a security audit. This ensures that the audit covers all relevant aspects of the security infrastructure and policies, allowing auditors to comprehensively assess the organization's adherence to security best practices and identify areas needing improvement.

Question 85

A company plans to validate the effectiveness of its newly implemented firewall. What is the best approach to test this?

- A) Performing a software update to ensure the firewall is running the latest version.
- B) Reviewing firewall logs manually for any unusual activity patterns.
- C) Conducting a series of controlled network penetration tests simulating external attacks.
- D) Running a vulnerability scan on the network to identify potential exploits.

Correct Answer: C

Explanation: Conducting a series of controlled network penetration tests to simulate external attacks is the best approach to test the effectiveness of a newly implemented firewall. This method directly assesses the firewall's ability to detect and block malicious traffic and attempts to breach network security, providing a practical evaluation of its performance in protecting the network.

Question 86

What is the primary role of a cyber insurance provider in the context of a data breach involving protected health information?

- A) Assessing the situation and coordinating with third-party forensics teams.
- B) Providing legal defense against claims arising from the breach.
- C) Negotiating ransom payments in cases of ransomware attacks.
- D) Direct reimbursement for financial losses incurred by affected customers.

Correct Answer: A

Explanation: The correct answer focuses on the immediate response required during a data breach, emphasizing the insurance provider's role in managing the crisis through technical and professional support, which is crucial for minimizing damage and navigating the complexities of data breaches.

Question 87

Fill in the blank: A comprehensive cyber insurance policy should include coverage for _____, which is essential for compensating third-party claims related to data breaches.

- A) regulatory fines and penalties
- B) compensation for public relations expenses
- C) loss of income due to business interruption
- D) restoration of damaged software systems

Correct Answer: A

Explanation: Regulatory fines and penalties can be a significant financial burden following data breaches, especially those involving sensitive information. A cyber insurance policy that covers these expenses is critical for financial protection and compliance with legal standards.

Question 88

A company is evaluating its cyber insurance needs. The policy it considers has exclusions for incidents involving outdated security software. Why is this problematic?

- A) It promotes better security practices among employees and contractors.
- B) It prevents the company from claiming losses due to non-compliance with software update policies.
- C) It allows the company to transfer the risk of software vulnerabilities to the insurer.
- D) It ensures that the insurance provider leads the incident response efforts.

Correct Answer: B

Explanation: Excluding coverage for incidents involving outdated security software places a heavy responsibility on the company to maintain rigorous update protocols. In the context of cyber insurance, such exclusions can lead to significant gaps in coverage, exposing the company to substantial financial risks if a breach occurs due to outdated software.

Question 89

During a cyber insurance policy audit, what would be a critical aspect to assess in ensuring the adequacy of coverage for a multinational corporation?

- A) Assessing the policy's compliance with international cybersecurity regulations.

- B) Checking the limits of indemnity per claim and in the aggregate.
- C) Evaluation of exclusions related to specific data types or geographies.
- D) The inclusion of coverage for attacks stemming from foreign nation-states.

Correct Answer: D

Explanation: For a multinational corporation, the threat of cyber-attacks originating from foreign nation-states represents a significant risk. Ensuring that the policy covers such attacks is essential for adequate protection against potentially devastating targeted breaches that could involve sophisticated threat actors.

Question 90

A software development firm wants to enhance its cyber risk management strategy. What type of additional coverage should it consider in its cyber insurance policy?

- A) Inclusion of coverage for intellectual property theft and source code breaches.
- B) Extension of the policy to include damages due to physical theft of data.
- C) Adding a clause for cyber defamation and social media risks.
- D) Coverage for loss of customer trust and subsequent business downturn.

Correct Answer: A

Explanation: As a software development firm, protection against intellectual property theft, especially source code breaches, is vital due to the potentially catastrophic impact on the company's competitive position and financial stability. Cyber insurance that covers this risk is an integral part of a comprehensive risk management strategy.

Question 91

What is the primary goal of a Red Team in a simulated cyber attack exercise?

- A) To evaluate the effectiveness of the organization's physical security controls.
- B) To test and improve the organization's defenses by simulating realistic cyber attacks.
- C) To create as much disruption as possible within the organization.
- D) To assess the response time of the IT support team during a breach.

Correct Answer: B

Explanation: The primary goal of a Red Team is to enhance an organization's cybersecurity posture by identifying weaknesses before they can be exploited by real attackers. This approach not only tests the effectiveness of existing defenses but also provides valuable insights into potential areas of improvement.

Question 92

Fill in the blank: During Blue Team evaluations, the main focus is on _____ to detect and respond to Red Team activities.

- A) conducting regular penetration testing on network systems
- B) enhancing system monitoring capabilities
- C) deploying additional antivirus solutions on critical servers
- D) updating firewall configurations regularly

Correct Answer: B

Explanation: Effective system monitoring is crucial for the Blue Team as it allows them to detect and respond to malicious activities promptly. Enhanced monitoring capabilities ensure that any anomalous behavior is quickly identified, providing a first line of defense against potential breaches.

Question 93

In a joint exercise, the Red Team successfully exploits a SQL injection flaw. What should the Blue Team prioritize in their response?

- A) Resetting all user passwords immediately to curb unauthorized access.
- B) Conducting a thorough analysis of the attack vectors and patching vulnerabilities.
- C) Revising security policies and protocols to reflect the new threat landscape.
- D) Isolating the affected systems to prevent further data leakage.

Correct Answer: B

Explanation: After a SQL injection attack, the immediate priority should be to understand how the breach occurred and to secure any vulnerabilities to prevent similar attacks. This involves a detailed analysis of attack methods used and swift remediation of the exploited vulnerabilities.

Question 94

A scenario involves a Red Team member gaining access through phishing. What should be the initial step for the Blue Team upon discovering this breach?

- A) Monitoring outgoing traffic to identify any data exfiltration attempts.
- B) Reviewing and updating incident response plans to better handle future attacks.
- C) Identifying the source and method of the phishing attack to prevent further incidents.
- D) Informing all employees about the breach to ensure widespread awareness.

Correct Answer: C

Explanation: Upon discovery of a phishing breach, it is essential for the Blue Team to first identify how the breach happened. This helps in understanding the attacker's methods and in taking measures to secure the vectors that were used for the attack, preventing further exploitation.

Question 95

During an exercise, the Red Team uses social engineering to access restricted areas. What is the most effective countermeasure for the Blue Team?

- A) Implementing strict access controls and continuous security awareness training.
- B) Conducting random security audits to check for any other vulnerabilities.
- C) Installing advanced intrusion detection systems across the network.
- D) Increasing surveillance and security personnel at key access points.

Correct Answer: A

Explanation: The most effective way to counteract social engineering attacks is by enforcing strict access controls combined with ongoing security training. This ensures that employees are aware of social engineering tactics and are equipped to resist them, while access controls limit the potential damage from breaches.

Question 96

What is a primary security measure for protecting OT networks against unauthorized access?

- A) Network segmentation to isolate operational systems from general IT networks.
- B) Installing antivirus software on all devices connected to the OT network.
- C) Regular password updates for all devices within the OT network.
- D) Implementing biometric access controls at all entry points to the facility.

Correct Answer: A

Explanation: Network segmentation is crucial in OT environments because it effectively limits access between less secure IT networks and critical operational systems, thereby reducing the attack surface and preventing potential intrusions from spreading across different network segments.

Question 97

Fill in the blank: To ensure the safety and reliability of operational systems, it is crucial to implement _____ controls.

- A) continuous vulnerability scanning
- B) regular data backup
- C) segregation of duties
- D) automated threat detection

Correct Answer: C

Explanation: Segregation of duties is vital to ensure that no single individual has the control necessary to both execute and cover up errors or fraud, especially in sensitive operational environments. This control is fundamental to maintaining the integrity and security of operational processes.

Question 98

In a scenario where an OT system is targeted by ransomware, what initial action should be taken to contain the attack?

- A) Disconnecting the OT network from the internet to reduce external access points.
- B) Running antivirus scans to remove the ransomware from affected systems.
- C) Immediately isolating affected systems to prevent the spread of the ransomware.
- D) Consulting with external cybersecurity experts to assess the situation.

Correct Answer: C

Explanation: When ransomware targets an OT system, the priority is to contain the attack to prevent further damage. Isolating affected systems helps to mitigate the spread of ransomware and provides time for a proper forensic analysis and recovery process without endangering unaffected parts of the network.

Question 99

During a routine security audit of an OT environment, discovering undocumented software on operational systems suggests what?

- A) A lack of compliance with standard operational procedures.
- B) Indications of efficient use of resources by optimizing software deployment.
- C) Signs of proactive maintenance and updates by the IT staff.
- D) Potential security risks due to unauthorized software that could be malicious.

Correct Answer: D

Explanation: Finding undocumented software during a security audit of OT systems often indicates unauthorized installations which can be a significant security risk, potentially introducing vulnerabilities or malicious functions designed to disrupt operational processes.

Question 100

What is the best practice for updating software on operational technology systems to maintain cybersecurity?

- A) Relying on automatic updates from software vendors without prior testing.
- B) Implementing a patch management policy that includes testing patches in a staging environment.
- C) Applying updates during regular business hours to minimize downtime.
- D) Manually updating software on each device individually to avoid errors.

Correct Answer: B

Explanation: Implementing a robust patch management policy that includes testing patches in a controlled staging environment before deployment in live OT environments is best practice. This method ensures compatibility and prevents the introduction of new vulnerabilities during the update process.

Question 101

When integrating cybersecurity awareness into an organization, which action would be most effective for a CISO to ensure staff compliance with updated security policies?

- A) Updating the company intranet with information on updated security protocols.
- B) Implementing an optional, rewards-based security awareness program.
- C) Sending out monthly newsletters highlighting recent security threats and tips.
- D) Conducting regular, mandatory training sessions and quizzes to reinforce policy knowledge.

Correct Answer: D

Explanation: Conducting regular, mandatory training sessions and quizzes is the most direct and measurable way to ensure that all employees are not only aware of but also understand the new and updated security policies. This approach helps in creating a security-conscious culture.

Question 102

A CISO reviews an incident report where sensitive data was leaked due to misconfigured access controls. What should be the primary focus of the post-incident analysis to prevent future occurrences?

- A) Focusing on training employees who failed to adhere to protocols.
- B) Assigning a temporary security manager to oversee the corrective actions.
- C) Increasing the budget for security tools and technologies.
- D) Evaluating the effectiveness of existing security controls and procedures in place.

Correct Answer: D

Explanation: The primary focus should be on evaluating existing security controls and procedures to identify why they failed to prevent unauthorized access. This evaluation helps in understanding the gaps in the current system and is essential for strengthening the security measures.

Question 103

Fill in the blank: A CISO implementing a new security framework should prioritize _____ to adapt security practices to the specific needs of the organization.

- A) customization of security measures
- B) reduction of staff to streamline security operations
- C) reliance on third-party security assessments
- D) centralized control over security decisions

Correct Answer: A

Explanation: Customization of security measures ensures that the security framework is tailored to fit the unique requirements and risks of the organization. This approach makes the security measures more effective as they address specific vulnerabilities and operational needs.

Question 104

In a simulated phishing attack orchestrated by a CISO, what metric should primarily be analyzed to assess the effectiveness of current training programs?

- A) The time it took to neutralize the phishing attack once detected.
- B) The total number of simulated phishing emails sent.
- C) The percentage of employees who reported the phishing attempt.

- D) The number of employees clicking on malicious links in the email.

Correct Answer: C

Explanation: Analyzing the percentage of employees who reported the phishing attempt provides insights into the alertness and preparedness of the workforce against actual phishing attacks. This metric is a direct indicator of the effectiveness of the current training programs on cybersecurity awareness.

Question 105

A CISO is considering new cybersecurity technologies to protect organizational assets. Which factor should be the priority when evaluating different options?

- A) The technology's ease of integration with existing systems.
- B) The cost of technology relative to the budget for cybersecurity.
- C) The scalability of the technology to accommodate future growth.
- D) The alignment of the technology with the organization's strategic security goals.

Correct Answer: D

Explanation: The alignment of new technology with the organization's strategic security goals is crucial as it ensures that the technology will support and enhance the existing security measures and not just add more complexity or redundancy to the system.

Question 106

What is the most effective way for a CISO to communicate the urgency of a cybersecurity threat to the board?

- A) Sending an email summary of the threat details without scheduling a meeting.
- B) Utilizing real-time data and recent examples to highlight potential impacts on the

business.
- C) Recommending immediate board approval for increased cybersecurity funding.
- D) Organizing a workshop with cybersecurity experts to educate the board about threats.

Correct Answer: B

Explanation: Utilizing real-time data and recent examples effectively communicates the immediacy and relevance of the threat. This approach ensures that the board can see the direct implications of cybersecurity issues on the business, aiding in swift decision-making.

Question 107

In preparing for a quarterly board meeting, what is the key focus a CISO should have when discussing upcoming cybersecurity initiatives?

- A) Focusing solely on the technical details of the cybersecurity tools being considered.
- B) Presenting the most recent cybersecurity audit findings in depth.
- C) Discussing only the budget requirements for the next fiscal year.
- D) Highlighting past successes and strategic alignment of proposed security initiatives.

Correct Answer: D

Explanation: Highlighting past successes and how the proposed initiatives align with the strategic goals of the company provides a compelling argument that these initiatives are both effective and essential for the organization's resilience against cyber threats.

Question 108

Fill in the blank: In board communications, a CISO should emphasize the _____ of cybersecurity investments to align with business objectives.

- A) Immediate cost savings

- B) Technical complexity
- C) Speed of implementation
- D) Return on investment

Correct Answer: D

Explanation: Emphasizing the return on investment from cybersecurity efforts helps in demonstrating how these investments protect not only the company's data but also its financial health, operational stability, and reputation, thus directly linking cybersecurity efforts to business value.

Question 109

During a crisis involving a data breach, how should a CISO update the board to maintain confidence and ensure transparent communication?

- A) Providing frequent updates with specific details on the steps being taken to mitigate the breach.
- B) Waiting to communicate until a full investigation has been completed.
- C) Sending a detailed written report after the crisis is resolved.
- D) Issuing a brief notice that the issue is being handled by the IT department.

Correct Answer: A

Explanation: Providing frequent and detailed updates during a data breach crisis helps maintain trust and transparency with the board. This approach ensures the board is continually informed of the situation and the measures taken, which is crucial for maintaining their confidence and support.

Question 110

A CISO plans to introduce a new security technology. Which approach should be used to present this to the board to gain their support?

- A) Showcasing endorsements from other industry leaders who have adopted the technology.
- B) Outlining the features of the technology without linking them to specific security threats.
- C) Demonstrating how the technology fits into the broader strategic context of the organization's security needs.
- D) Comparing the costs and benefits of the new technology with those of existing solutions.

Correct Answer: C

Explanation: Demonstrating how new technology aligns with the organization's overall security strategy and needs allows the board to understand its value and relevance, thereby facilitating informed decision-making and support for the investment.

Question 111

In a cybersecurity incident, which action best demonstrates ethical leadership when managing a team responsible for data breach analysis?

- A) Issue a memo reprimanding the involved team members without further investigation.
- B) Privately dismiss the team members believed to be most responsible.
- C) Initiate an impartial investigation, ensuring the process is transparent to all stakeholders.
- D) Directly involve law enforcement without a preliminary internal review.

Correct Answer: C

Explanation: Ethical leadership in cybersecurity emphasizes accountability and transparency. By initiating an impartial investigation and keeping the process open, leaders uphold both ethical standards and foster trust within the team and external stakeholders.

Question 112

Fill in the blank: The principle of _____ requires cybersecurity leaders to avoid conflicts of interest and ensure their decisions are made based on the security and welfare of their organization.

- A) duty of diligence
- B) duty of loyalty
- C) duty of care
- D) duty of confidentiality

Correct Answer: B

Explanation: The 'duty of loyalty' requires leaders to prioritize the interests of their organization above personal gains or external pressures. This principle is fundamental in making unbiased decisions that enhance organizational security and integrity.

Question 113

A cybersecurity manager discovers that an employee has used unauthorized software to bypass security protocols. What is the most ethical first step in addressing this issue?

- A) Ignore the issue to avoid internal conflict and possible reprisals against the employee.
- B) Conduct an internal seminar about the legal implications of bypassing security protocols.
- C) Schedule a private meeting with the employee to understand their motivations and discuss the consequences.
- D) Publicly reprimand the employee to deter others from similar actions.

Correct Answer: C

Explanation: Addressing the employee's actions directly and privately respects their dignity and provides a constructive environment to address misconduct. This approach not only helps in understanding the root cause but also reinforces ethical standards within the team.

Question 114

Consider a scenario where a cybersecurity leader must decide on reporting an unintentional violation of data privacy laws to a regulatory body. Which option aligns best with ethical leadership?

- A) Consult with other managers to form a consensus before making a decision.
- B) Report the violation promptly to demonstrate compliance and transparency.
- C) Decide not to report the violation to protect the company's public image.
- D) Wait until the annual audit to disclose the violation in the regular report.

Correct Answer: B

Explanation: Ethical leadership necessitates transparency and compliance with legal standards. Promptly reporting an unintentional violation demonstrates a commitment to ethical practices and legal compliance, building trust with regulatory bodies and maintaining the organization's reputation.

Question 115

During an ethical hacking exercise, it is found that a critical vulnerability could potentially expose customer data. How should the leader ensure the exercise continues ethically?

- A) Inform the client of the potential risk immediately and recommend pausing the exercise.
- B) Continue the exercise as planned without informing the client, noting to fix it later.
- C) Cover up the finding until the end of the exercise to maintain the testing schedule.
- D) Delay reporting until a solution is developed to mitigate the vulnerability.

Correct Answer: A

Explanation: Immediately informing the client about a critical vulnerability during an ethical hacking exercise exemplifies responsible and ethical conduct. This decision prioritizes client security and trust over project timelines or potential embarrassment, aligning with the highest ethical standards.

Question 116

During a negotiation with a vendor over a cybersecurity tool, the vendor offers a price reduction if certain security features are removed. How should the cybersecurity leader respond to ensure a balanced agreement?

- A) Politely decline the offer, insisting that the security features are critical to the organization's needs.
- B) Accept the price reduction as a means of staying within the department's budget.
- C) Accept the offer and rely on internal teams to compensate for the lack of security features.
- D) Counteroffer for a slightly higher price with the critical security features included.

Correct Answer: A

Explanation: Declining the vendor's offer for a price reduction in exchange for removing security features protects the organization's cybersecurity posture. Prioritizing security over cost ensures that the integrity of the systems remains intact, avoiding potential vulnerabilities or compliance failures that could arise from reduced security capabilities.

Question 117

Fill in the blank: Effective negotiation in cybersecurity requires _____ to maintain open communication and mutual trust between internal teams and vendors.

- A) a clear strategy
- B) a flexible approach

- C) a defensive posture
- D) an aggressive tactic

Correct Answer: A

Explanation: A clear strategy in negotiations is essential for maintaining focus on the organization's security needs while fostering open communication and trust with the vendor. A well-defined approach ensures that both sides understand their responsibilities, leading to a more effective and secure outcome for the organization.

Question 118

A vendor is pushing for a fast agreement on a security service contract that doesn't include critical service level agreements (SLAs). What is the most ethical approach to negotiating this contract?

- A) Insist that the SLAs must be included and take the necessary time to review the terms carefully.
- B) Sign the contract and attempt to negotiate the SLAs after the agreement is finalized.
- C) Agree to the terms but request a discount due to the lack of SLAs in the agreement.
- D) Allow the fast agreement but include a verbal agreement to revisit the SLAs at a later date.

Correct Answer: A

Explanation: Insisting on the inclusion of critical SLAs in a contract demonstrates a cybersecurity leader's commitment to ethical negotiations. By ensuring the necessary time is taken to review the terms, the leader prioritizes the long-term security of the organization over short-term convenience, avoiding potential risks from inadequate service provisions.

Question 119

In a scenario where internal teams are pressuring to finalize a vendor contract quickly, but certain compliance checks haven't been completed, how should the cybersecurity leader handle the negotiation?

- A) Press for faster internal compliance checks to meet the urgency of the internal teams.
- B) Proceed with the contract and address any compliance concerns after the signing.
- C) Finalize the contract under the condition that compliance can be verified later.
- D) Ensure that all compliance checks are completed before proceeding with any contractual agreement.

Correct Answer: D

Explanation: Ensuring that compliance checks are completed before finalizing a contract shows a firm stance on maintaining regulatory requirements and organizational security standards. This approach avoids rushing into agreements that may compromise the organization's legal obligations or security posture.

Question 120

Consider a situation where a vendor refuses to provide full transparency on their incident response times. What approach should the cybersecurity leader take in this negotiation to protect organizational interests?

- A) Accept the vendor's refusal and adjust internal incident response protocols to account for the lack of transparency.
- B) Demand that the vendor provides full transparency or negotiate for stronger incident response guarantees.
- C) Allow the vendor to maintain some privacy and work around the limited information on incident response.
- D) Negotiate for longer-term transparency agreements instead of focusing on incident response times.

Correct Answer: B

Explanation: Demanding full transparency from the vendor regarding incident response times safeguards the organization's interests. This negotiation approach ensures that the vendor is held accountable for their services, and the organization can rely on the vendor's support during security incidents, reducing potential risks from unaddressed vulnerabilities.

Question 121

A security manager is leading a meeting to discuss how employees can integrate security best practices into their daily routines. What is the best way for the manager to promote a culture of security during this meeting?

- A) Present statistics on data breaches and explain the technical side of each incident.
- B) Direct employees to detailed documentation on the company's security policies.
- C) Encourage employees to share real-world examples of how breaches impact their personal and professional lives.
- D) Focus on the legal requirements for security compliance, citing specific regulations.

Correct Answer: C

Explanation: By encouraging employees to share real-world examples, the manager can make security issues feel more personal and relatable, which helps employees understand the impact of security breaches. This approach fosters engagement and reinforces a culture of security by showing that cybersecurity is not just an abstract concept, but something that affects them directly.

Question 122

Fill in the blank: To build a strong security culture, it is essential to _____ throughout the organization, ensuring that all employees understand their role in protecting sensitive information.

- A) promote ongoing security training
- B) emphasize security audits
- C) establish mandatory performance reviews

- D) enforce strict compliance policies

Correct Answer: A

Explanation: Promoting ongoing security training ensures that employees are continually updated on the latest threats and best practices. This approach creates a proactive security culture where everyone is informed, aware, and ready to contribute to maintaining the organization's security posture.

Question 123

In a scenario where an employee consistently bypasses security procedures to increase their productivity, how should the security leader address this behavior while promoting a security-conscious culture?

- A) Publicly reprimand the employee to set an example for others who may attempt to bypass protocols.
- B) Automate the process so employees cannot bypass security protocols, removing their responsibility for security decisions.
- C) Have a private discussion with the employee to understand their motivations and explain how their actions endanger the organization.
- D) Suggest to the employee that bypassing security can be tolerated under tight deadlines but not on a regular basis.

Correct Answer: C

Explanation: A private discussion with the employee addresses the issue without creating a negative environment. This approach respects the employee while also reinforcing the importance of adhering to security protocols. It provides an opportunity for the leader to educate the employee about the broader impact of their actions on organizational security.

Question 124

During a cybersecurity awareness training session, several employees express frustration about the inconvenience of security protocols. How should the trainer respond to promote security culture without discouraging participation?

- A) Increase the technical complexity of the training to demonstrate the importance of strict compliance.
- B) Stop the training and reschedule it to address the employees' frustrations individually.
- C) Ignore the complaints and continue the training session without addressing the concerns.
- D) Acknowledge the concerns but emphasize how security measures protect both the organization and employees.

Correct Answer: D

Explanation: Acknowledging the concerns while emphasizing the protective benefits of security measures strikes a balance between understanding the employees' frustrations and reinforcing the importance of cybersecurity. This approach maintains engagement and shows that security protocols are designed for the benefit of both the organization and its employees, fostering a positive security culture.

Question 125

A company is rolling out a new password policy that requires more complex passwords and frequent updates. Some employees are resistant to the change. How can the security team effectively implement the policy while fostering a positive security culture?

- A) Offer clear communication about the reasons for the change and provide easy-to-follow guidelines for creating strong passwords.
- B) Require immediate compliance and implement disciplinary measures for employees who resist the policy.
- C) Adjust the password policy to make it less strict to accommodate the employees' frustrations.
- D) Give employees full autonomy to choose their own password policies as long as they meet minimum security standards.

Correct Answer: A

Explanation: Offering clear communication and easy-to-follow guidelines helps employees understand why the password policy is necessary. This approach reduces resistance by making the process straightforward and ensuring that employees feel supported during the transition, which ultimately fosters a more cooperative and secure environment.

Question 126

A cybersecurity team is struggling with communication issues during incident response exercises. As the team leader, what is the most effective step you can take to improve communication and ensure the team operates efficiently?

- A) Conduct a debriefing after every exercise and encourage open feedback to address communication challenges.
- B) Assign roles more clearly to avoid any confusion during future exercises and limit communication to key channels.
- C) Limit the number of people allowed to speak during exercises to prevent overwhelming team members.
- D) Use pre-defined scripts for communication during incident response exercises to streamline the process.

Correct Answer: A

Explanation: Conducting a debriefing after every exercise allows team members to reflect on what worked and what didn't in terms of communication. Open feedback helps identify specific communication issues and encourages team members to voice their thoughts, leading to a more collaborative environment and improved performance.

Question 127

Fill in the blank: A cybersecurity team leader should promote _____ to encourage collaboration and maintain high morale within the team.

- A) rigid performance metrics
- B) strict hierarchical control
- C) strict supervision from leadership
- D) transparency and openness

Correct Answer: D

Explanation: Transparency and openness are essential for fostering a positive team environment. By promoting these values, the leader ensures that team members feel comfortable sharing ideas, collaborating, and addressing challenges, which leads to a more cohesive and motivated cybersecurity team.

Question 128

A new cybersecurity analyst on the team consistently fails to follow established protocols during security audits. As the team leader, what is the most appropriate course of action to correct this behavior and improve team performance?

- A) Assign a senior member to monitor the analyst during audits and report any issues.
- B) Reduce the analyst's responsibilities and reassign critical tasks to more experienced team members.
- C) Schedule a private meeting with the analyst to provide constructive feedback and offer additional training.
- D) Publicly address the analyst's failures in the next team meeting to set an example for others.

Correct Answer: C

Explanation: Scheduling a private meeting with the analyst allows the team leader to provide personalized feedback without embarrassing the employee in front of the team. Offering additional training shows a commitment to the analyst's growth and ensures that future audits are conducted in line with team protocols.

Question 129

During a major security breach, two senior members of your cybersecurity team disagree on the best course of action. How should you, as the team leader, handle this situation to maintain team cohesion and ensure the breach is resolved efficiently?

- A) Take a hands-off approach and allow the team to resolve the disagreement on their own.
- B) Make an immediate decision without involving the team to avoid further delays in addressing the breach.
- C) Allow both members to argue their cases in front of the team to reach a democratic decision on the next steps.
- D) Facilitate a meeting where both members present their views, then make a final decision based on the most sound technical reasoning.

Correct Answer: D

Explanation: Facilitating a discussion where both members present their views allows the team leader to understand the technical reasoning behind each position. Making a final decision based on sound reasoning helps maintain team cohesion, as it shows the leader is fair and focused on resolving the breach efficiently.

Question 130

A cybersecurity team is responsible for managing several critical systems, but the workload is becoming overwhelming. How should the team leader prioritize tasks to ensure that the most important systems remain secure while preventing team burnout?

- A) Bring in an external contractor to handle some of the critical systems while allowing the team to manage the others.
- B) Suspend the less important systems until the team has the bandwidth to handle the remaining workload.
- C) Assign all critical tasks to senior members and reduce the workload for junior team members until the breach is resolved.
- D) Reevaluate the workload and delegate the most critical systems to the senior members while distributing other tasks evenly across the team.

Correct Answer: D

Explanation: Reevaluating the workload and delegating critical systems to the most experienced team members helps ensure that important tasks are handled properly. Distributing other tasks evenly prevents burnout among the team while maintaining focus on securing the most vital systems.

Question 131

During a cybersecurity incident involving employee data, which department should the security team collaborate with to ensure compliance with privacy regulations and internal policies?

- A) Work with the legal department to ensure privacy laws are followed and employee data is handled securely.
- B) Communicate directly with senior management and bypass other departments to handle the incident independently.
- C) Collaborate with the marketing department to ensure the public messaging around the incident is accurate.
- D) Coordinate with the finance department to ensure the costs related to the incident response are properly allocated.

Correct Answer: A

Explanation: Collaborating with the legal department ensures that privacy regulations are adhered to during a cybersecurity incident involving employee data. This collaboration helps to ensure that employee data is handled appropriately, in line with legal obligations, while mitigating potential legal risks for the organization.

Question 132

Fill in the blank: When handling an insider threat investigation, it is important for the cybersecurity team to work closely with _____ to ensure that the investigation adheres to legal standards and protects employee rights.

- A) the marketing department
- B) the operations department
- C) the finance department
- D) the legal department

Correct Answer: D

Explanation: The legal department is crucial when conducting insider threat investigations to ensure the process complies with legal standards and protects employee rights. This collaboration ensures that evidence is collected and handled properly, and that the investigation aligns with both legal and organizational policies.

Question 133

A cybersecurity manager is working with the legal department on a potential data breach that may lead to regulatory penalties. What is the most appropriate first step for the cybersecurity manager to ensure the legal team has the necessary information?

- A) Wait for legal to request specific information before sharing details about the incident.
- B) Provide detailed logs and records related to the incident, ensuring all relevant data is shared transparently with the legal team.
- C) Immediately notify external auditors and provide them with the necessary information before involving the legal team.
- D) Focus on containing the breach internally before engaging the legal team to avoid potential legal repercussions.

Correct Answer: B

Explanation: Providing detailed logs and records to the legal team is a proactive approach that ensures all relevant data related to a potential breach is available. This allows the legal department to assess regulatory risks, ensuring the organization can address any legal ramifications of the breach in a timely manner.

Question 134

During the onboarding of new employees, the HR department requests assistance from the cybersecurity team to educate staff on security policies. How should the cybersecurity team collaborate with HR to ensure that the security training is effective and aligned with organizational goals?

- A) Conduct a one-time security training session that focuses on technical procedures without involving HR.
- B) Send a memo outlining the basic security policies for HR to distribute during the onboarding process.
- C) Design an independent security training for employees without HR involvement and deliver it via online modules.
- D) Develop a training program that highlights key security practices while aligning with HR's employee engagement strategies.

Correct Answer: D

Explanation: Developing a training program in collaboration with HR ensures that the cybersecurity training is not only technically accurate but also engaging and aligned with the organization's goals for employee development. This approach increases the effectiveness of the training by ensuring it resonates with employees and meets organizational standards.

Question 135

In a scenario where the IT department and the legal team have differing priorities regarding the timeline for implementing new security controls, how should the cybersecurity manager manage this cross-departmental conflict while ensuring organizational security is not compromised?

- A) Defer to the legal department's timeline, as they are responsible for regulatory

compliance.
- B) Facilitate a meeting where both departments discuss their concerns, then prioritize security needs based on risk assessment.
- C) Allow both teams to follow their own timelines and resolve the security controls at their own pace.
- D) Allow IT to proceed with the timeline, as their role in implementing security measures is most critical to the organization.

Correct Answer: B

Explanation: Facilitating a meeting between IT and the legal team to discuss their priorities and using risk assessment as the basis for decision-making allows the cybersecurity manager to mediate the conflict while ensuring security needs are met. This approach balances the urgency of security controls with legal compliance, protecting the organization from both technical and regulatory risks.

Question 136

During an incident response simulation, a security team is required to identify and mitigate a simulated ransomware attack. What should be the initial step in handling this scenario?

- A) Isolating affected systems to prevent the spread of the malware
- B) Running antivirus scans on all workstations to find malicious software
- C) Paying the ransom to quickly regain access to the encrypted files
- D) Deleting all files suspected to be encrypted by the ransomware

Correct Answer: A

Explanation: Isolating the affected systems is crucial to limit the spread of the malware during a ransomware attack. This step ensures that the malware does not propagate across the network, securing critical systems while the team assesses the situation and plans further mitigation strategies.

Question 137

What type of attack involves malicious individuals attempting to enter a restricted area by following an employee with access, without being noticed?

- A) Phishing, where attackers trick someone into giving them confidential information
- B) Vishing, using the telephone system to trick people into disclosing secure information
- C) Tailgating, an unauthorized person following someone with access to secure areas
- D) Baiting, where attackers leave malware-infected physical devices in accessible areas

Correct Answer: C

Explanation: Tailgating is a security threat where an unauthorized individual gains access to restricted areas by following an authorized person. This scenario often occurs without the notice of the legitimate access holder, posing a significant security risk that training simulations aim to address.

Question 138

Fill in the blank: The most effective method to train a new security analyst on network monitoring tools is through _____.

- A) weekly theoretical courses that include quizzes on what was covered
- B) monthly webinars by external experts discussing recent threats
- C) reading comprehensive manuals and documents about the software without guidance
- D) supervised hands-on sessions to ensure practical experience

Correct Answer: D

Explanation: Supervised hands-on sessions provide practical experience and immediate feedback, which is critical for effectively learning how to use network monitoring tools. This approach helps reinforce theoretical knowledge through real-world application, ensuring that the analyst is well-prepared to handle actual security incidents.

Question 139

In a phishing attack simulation, trainees must decide how to respond to a suspicious email claiming to be from a trusted vendor. What is the best course of action?

- A) Forward the email to colleagues to see if they received a similar message
- B) Ignore the email completely and do not inform IT department about the received message
- C) Verify the sender's email address and look for signs of phishing before responding
- D) Click on the link provided to see if it redirects to the vendor's official page

Correct Answer: C

Explanation: Verifying the sender's email address and looking for signs of phishing are essential steps in responding to suspicious emails. This action helps in identifying potential threats and teaches trainees to exercise caution, promoting best practices in handling email-based security incidents.

Question 140

A company plans a drill that simulates an SQL injection in their test environment. Which technique should the security team use to detect and mitigate the threat effectively?

- A) Using parameterized queries that can prevent the execution of part of the SQL code as a command
- B) Applying regular updates to the database management system to avoid known vulnerabilities
- C) Conducting regular security audits to check for misconfigurations or outdated software
- D) Employing intrusion detection systems that alert on unusual database activities

Correct Answer: A

Explanation: Parameterized queries are a method of preventing SQL injection attacks by separating SQL code from data inputs. This technique ensures that user inputs are treated as data rather than executable code, effectively mitigating the risk of unauthorized database commands being run during a simulation exercise.

Question 141

What strategy should be employed first when a security team detects unauthorized access to sensitive data?

- A) Conducting an IT audit to review all recent access logs and system changes
- B) Encryption of all data to prevent further unauthorized access while investigating
- C) Immediate temporary suspension of suspected accounts to limit further unauthorized access
- D) Public announcement to the company about the breach to ensure transparency

Correct Answer: C

Explanation: Temporarily suspending the suspected accounts quickly limits the potential for further unauthorized access, securing the data and systems while a thorough investigation is conducted. This step is essential in controlling the situation and preventing further damage while the incident is assessed.

Question 142

Which monitoring tool is most effective for identifying unusual user behavior that could indicate an insider threat?

- A) Installation of CCTV cameras in key areas to monitor physical access to servers
- B) Implementation of a strict key card access system for entering server rooms
- C) Deployment of antivirus software across all endpoints to detect potential malicious activities
- D) User and Entity Behavior Analytics (UEBA) systems for advanced behavior pattern recognition

Correct Answer: D

Explanation: UEBA systems are designed to identify deviations from normal user behavior patterns, making them highly effective for spotting potential insider threats. These systems analyze historical data to establish baselines and flag unusual activities, which is crucial in early detection of malicious actions by insiders.

Question 143

Fill in the blank: Regular _____ are crucial for detecting changes in user behavior that may signal an insider threat.

- A) monthly security awareness training sessions
- B) audits of access logs and user activity
- C) weekly team meetings to discuss security concerns and updates
- D) biannual password update mandates

Correct Answer: B

Explanation: Regular audits of access logs and user activity are essential for detecting unauthorized access or anomalous behavior that may indicate an insider threat. This proactive approach helps in identifying potential security breaches early, allowing timely intervention.

Question 144

In a scenario where an employee is suspected of leaking confidential data, what initial action should be taken?

- A) Immediate termination of the employee to prevent further data leakage
- B) Isolate the employee's access to sensitive information while the investigation is

underway
- C) Counseling session with the employee to understand their actions and motivations
- D) Legal action against the employee based on the evidence gathered so far

Correct Answer: B

Explanation: Isolating the employee's access to sensitive information is a critical first step in managing suspected data leaks. It ensures that the risk of further data exposure is minimized while a detailed investigation is carried out to confirm the breach and identify the extent of the leak.

Question 145

A security analyst discovers a potential insider trading confidential company information. What is the first step in the investigation process?

- A) Conducting a preliminary review of the employee's email and communication records
- B) Engage external cybersecurity consultants to conduct an independent review
- C) Running a full network scan to identify any external breaches linked to the insider
- D) Setting up a honeypot to attract and identify malicious insider activity

Correct Answer: A

Explanation: Conducting a preliminary review of the suspect's email and communication records is a direct method to gather evidence and assess the nature of the information being shared. This step is vital in establishing a timeline and context for the suspected insider trading activities, providing critical insights for the ongoing investigation.

Question 146

What is the most effective method for a CISO to manage stress during a major security breach?

- A) Focus solely on technical details and avoid communicating with the team
- B) Ignore less significant security alerts to focus on the major breach only
- C) Take personal charge of all tasks to ensure everything is done correctly
- D) Prioritize tasks based on impact and urgency while delegating non-critical tasks

Correct Answer: D

Explanation: Prioritizing tasks based on their impact and urgency while delegating non-essential tasks helps maintain focus on critical issues without being overwhelmed. This method ensures that the most pressing issues are addressed promptly while allowing the CISO to manage their stress by not being bogged down with less critical details.

Question 147

Which approach should a security manager take to effectively reduce stress when overseeing multiple security projects?

- A) Implement a clear communication plan that involves regular updates from project leads
- B) Increase working hours to monitor the progress of each project personally
- C) Outsource some of the security tasks to reduce the workload temporarily
- D) Conduct daily stress-relief activities with the team to boost morale

Correct Answer: A

Explanation: A clear communication plan with regular updates from project leads keeps the security manager well-informed and reduces the stress of uncertainty. This structure helps in managing multiple projects by ensuring that all team members are aligned and that there is continuous progress monitoring without the need for the manager to be involved in every minute detail.

Question 148

Fill in the blank: To alleviate stress, a Chief Security Officer should prioritize _____ in their daily routine.

- A) regular check-ins with each team member
- B) time for strategic planning and reflection
- C) physical workouts early in the morning
- D) updates on cybersecurity trends

Correct Answer: B

Explanation: Incorporating time for strategic planning and reflection in a daily routine helps Chief Security Officers to focus on long-term goals and the broader security landscape, rather than getting lost in day-to-day reactive measures. This practice can significantly reduce stress by providing a clearer sense of control and direction.

Question 149

During a severe network attack, what should the IT security chief do first to manage their stress and maintain clear decision-making?

- A) Call an impromptu meeting of all staff to brainstorm solutions
- B) Immediately start micromanaging each team's response efforts
- C) Dive directly into solving the technical issues without preliminary assessments
- D) Take a moment to perform a brief mindfulness exercise to regain focus

Correct Answer: D

Explanation: Performing a brief mindfulness exercise during high-stress situations like a severe network attack can significantly aid in stress management. This practice helps in clearing the mind, refocusing on the present, and maintaining calm, which is crucial for making clear and effective decisions under pressure.

Question 150

A security director receives simultaneous alerts of data breaches in several departments. What is the best initial action to manage both the situation and their stress?

- A) Request immediate external cybersecurity assistance before assessing the situation
- B) Begin by isolating the network sections reported to have breaches
- C) Establish a central command center to coordinate responses and gather data
- D) Send out a company-wide email demanding updates from all departments

Correct Answer: C

Explanation: Establishing a central command center immediately after receiving multiple breach alerts helps to organize the influx of information and coordinate a controlled, effective response. This approach not only aids in handling the incidents efficiently but also significantly reduces stress by centralizing command and control, ensuring that efforts are not duplicated and resources are used effectively.

Question 151

Which encryption algorithm should be selected to ensure both strong security and fast performance when encrypting large volumes of data?

- A) Advanced Encryption Standard (AES) with 256-bit keys for high security and efficient performance
- B) Rivest Cipher 4 (RC4) with a 128-bit key for faster processing of streaming data
- C) Data Encryption Standard (DES) for simplicity and quicker encryption of small files
- D) Triple DES (3DES) for enhanced security of confidential but smaller datasets

Correct Answer: A

Explanation: Advanced Encryption Standard (AES) with 256-bit keys provides a high level of security and is widely recognized for its balance between strength and efficiency, making it ideal for encrypting large amounts of data. It ensures robust encryption while still allowing for relatively fast processing, making it the preferred choice for most enterprise-level encryption needs.

Question 152

What is the best way to securely manage encryption keys for a small to medium-sized enterprise using encryption across multiple platforms?

- A) Use password-protected spreadsheets to store encryption keys for all platforms
- B) Use third-party services to generate and store encryption keys on demand
- C) Store encryption keys locally on each device for easy access during encryption tasks
- D) A centralized key management system with automatic key rotation and strict access controls

Correct Answer: D

Explanation: A centralized key management system with automatic key rotation ensures that encryption keys are securely managed across platforms, reducing the risk of compromise. This approach simplifies key management by providing a single, secure repository for keys, while automatic rotation ensures that old keys are periodically replaced to further enhance security.

Question 153

Fill in the blank: When using symmetric encryption, both the sender and recipient must securely exchange _____.

- A) session tokens to establish secure connections during encrypted communications
- B) hash values to validate data integrity during transmission
- C) digital signatures to authenticate the sender's identity
- D) encryption keys through a secure channel

Correct Answer: D

Explanation: In symmetric encryption, both the sender and recipient must securely exchange encryption keys, as they are the same for both encryption and decryption. Secure key exchange is essential to ensure that unauthorized parties do not intercept or compromise the keys, which would allow them to decrypt the data.

Question 154

During a security assessment, you discover that sensitive emails are being sent without encryption. What is the first step the security team should take to enforce encryption across email communications?

- A) Require employees to manually encrypt emails using public key encryption before sending
- B) Perform regular manual checks of emails sent by employees to ensure encryption is used
- C) Implement a company-wide email encryption policy that requires encryption for all outgoing sensitive emails
- D) Send an email reminder about the importance of encrypting emails before sending them

Correct Answer: C

Explanation: Implementing a company-wide email encryption policy ensures that all employees follow standardized practices for encrypting sensitive information. By enforcing encryption across email communications, the security team can mitigate risks related to data breaches and protect sensitive information from unauthorized access during transmission.

Question 155

A security administrator needs to encrypt backups of large databases stored in the cloud. Which encryption approach should be used to ensure maximum protection without compromising system performance?

- A) Full-disk encryption on the database server without any additional cloud encryption
- B) Server-side encryption provided by the cloud provider with client-side key management for extra security
- C) Rely entirely on cloud provider's built-in encryption with no additional key management
- D) Hybrid encryption methods using RSA for key exchange and AES for encrypting the database content

Correct Answer: B

Explanation: Server-side encryption provided by the cloud provider, combined with client-side key management, offers a strong layer of protection by ensuring that only authorized users can access the encrypted data. This approach allows the cloud provider to handle the heavy encryption workload while ensuring that the customer retains control over the encryption keys, providing both security and performance optimization.

Question 156

What is the most effective way to implement multifactor authentication (MFA) for remote workers accessing sensitive systems?

- A) Deploy biometrics exclusively to authenticate remote workers, removing the need for passwords
- B) Use email-based authentication codes for users who cannot access their primary MFA method
- C) Require hardware tokens in combination with a password for secure authentication
- D) Use SMS-based codes as a second factor for quick setup and easy deployment

Correct Answer: C

Explanation: Requiring hardware tokens in combination with a password is one of the most secure ways to implement MFA for remote workers. Hardware tokens generate unique, time-sensitive codes that significantly reduce the risk of account compromise, while passwords ensure an additional layer of security.

Question 157

What should be the first step when deploying MFA across an organization to protect all employee accounts?

- A) Conduct a company-wide audit of all user accounts before implementing any MFA solution
- B) Enforce MFA only for privileged accounts with access to administrative tools
- C) Deploy MFA immediately for all accounts without prior communication or training
- D) Conduct a comprehensive risk assessment to determine which systems require MFA first

Correct Answer: D

Explanation: Conducting a comprehensive risk assessment is a critical first step in deploying MFA across an organization. This process identifies the most vulnerable systems and accounts that need immediate protection, ensuring a strategic and effective rollout that prioritizes the most critical assets.

Question 158

Fill in the blank: The most secure combination for MFA includes something the user knows, something the user has, and _____.

- A) something related to the time of login to verify user activity patterns
- B) something based on recent activity logs to ensure account protection
- C) something related to the user's IP address for added location-based security
- D) something the user is, such as biometric data

Correct Answer: D

Explanation: Something the user is, such as biometric data (e.g., fingerprints or facial recognition), adds a unique and highly secure layer to multifactor authentication. This factor is hard to replicate or steal, making it a vital component in securing user accounts in combination with knowledge-based or possession-based factors.

Question 159

During an MFA rollout, a company faces pushback from employees about usability concerns. What approach should IT take to ensure successful adoption while maintaining security?

- A) Relax MFA requirements for low-risk systems to reduce complexity for end users
- B) Delay MFA rollout to avoid disrupting business operations until all concerns are resolved
- C) Provide user training on the benefits and convenience of MFA, while offering flexible authentication methods
- D) Allow users to opt out of MFA if they experience difficulties

Correct Answer: C

Explanation: Providing user training on the benefits and convenience of MFA, while offering flexible authentication methods, addresses employee concerns about usability. When users understand the importance of MFA and have options such as mobile apps, hardware tokens, or biometrics, they are more likely to adopt the system.

Question 160

A large enterprise wants to implement MFA for both on-premises and cloud services. Which method should the security team choose to streamline MFA across different platforms without sacrificing security?

- A) Rely solely on password managers for internal systems and MFA for external access points
- B) Implement MFA only for cloud services while keeping internal systems on password-only authentication
- C) Implement a unified MFA solution that integrates with both cloud and on-premises

systems
- D) Set up separate MFA systems for cloud applications and on-premises resources to prevent integration issues

Correct Answer: C

Explanation: Implementing a unified MFA solution that integrates with both cloud and on-premises systems simplifies the security management process and ensures consistent protection across all platforms. This approach reduces complexity while maintaining strong security controls, making it easier to manage authentication for large enterprises.

Question 161

When using a SIEM tool to detect suspicious activity in real time, what is the most effective first step to take after a potential threat is flagged?

- A) Immediately block the source IP without further investigation to prevent any potential breach
- B) Run a full system scan to check for malware infections linked to the flagged activity
- C) Notify all relevant employees about the detected threat to prevent further exposure
- D) Investigate the source IP and check if it matches known malicious addresses from threat intelligence feeds

Correct Answer: D

Explanation: Investigating the source IP and checking if it matches known malicious addresses from threat intelligence feeds is an effective first step when a potential threat is flagged in a SIEM tool. This method helps the security team quickly determine if the detected activity is linked to previously identified malicious actors, guiding further response actions.

Question 162

What is the key advantage of using a SIEM platform to aggregate logs from multiple devices across the network?

- A) It improves visibility of traffic on each device by encrypting log data
- B) It helps reduce storage space by filtering out less important logs from the system
- C) It centralizes log collection, making it easier to detect patterns and anomalies across different systems
- D) It increases processing speed by filtering out redundant logs before analysis

Correct Answer: C

Explanation: Centralizing log collection is a key advantage of using a SIEM platform because it allows the security team to detect patterns and anomalies across a wide range of systems and devices. This broad visibility is essential for identifying and responding to security incidents that may not be evident when monitoring individual systems in isolation.

Question 163

Fill in the blank: One of the most important features of a SIEM tool is _____, which allows analysts to correlate data from different sources to identify security events.

- A) firewall integration that enhances network defense by actively blocking malicious traffic
- B) event correlation that links related security alerts across multiple platforms
- C) file integrity monitoring that tracks changes to critical files within the system
- D) tokenization to secure sensitive data before processing it in the system

Correct Answer: B

Explanation: Event correlation is one of the most critical features of a SIEM tool, as it links data from different sources to help analysts recognize related security events. This function allows security teams to detect complex threats that may involve multiple systems and trigger separate alerts, enhancing overall threat detection and response.

Question 164

A security team detects unusual login attempts from multiple geographic locations on an employee's account through their SIEM dashboard. What should be the next step in investigating this suspicious activity?

- A) Review the event correlation logs in the SIEM tool to identify any patterns of previous suspicious behavior
- B) Isolate the employee's device from the network to prevent further attacks
- C) Perform a vulnerability scan on the employee's device to check for malware
- D) Disable the employee's account and escalate the issue to senior management for further analysis

Correct Answer: A

Explanation: Reviewing the event correlation logs in the SIEM tool is the next logical step in investigating suspicious login attempts from multiple locations. These logs provide a historical view of related security events, helping the security team identify patterns of previous suspicious behavior and determine if the login activity is part of a larger attack.

Question 165

During a forensic investigation, an organization uses a SIEM tool to analyze logs and trace the origin of a malware infection. Which SIEM feature is most useful in helping to pinpoint the source of the attack?

- A) Log retention and analysis to review historical data for evidence of initial malware entry
- B) Geo-location tracking to determine the physical location of the attacker during the breach
- C) Real-time alerts that notify the security team of ongoing threats as they occur
- D) Anomaly detection to identify irregular activity patterns in the network

Correct Answer: A

Explanation: Log retention and analysis are crucial for forensic investigations, especially when tracing the origin of a malware infection. SIEM tools store large amounts of log data, allowing analysts to go back in time and review historical records to find clues about the initial entry point of the malware and understand how it spread through the network.

Question 166

What is a crucial step in preserving digital evidence when starting a forensic investigation after a security breach?

- A) Running antivirus scans to remove any traces of malware from the systems.
- B) Disconnecting the power of affected devices to preserve the current state of volatile memory.
- C) Ensuring the physical security of the systems involved to prevent further access or tampering.
- D) Immediately creating backups of affected systems to ensure data recovery.

Correct Answer: C

Explanation: Ensuring the physical security of the system is essential as it prevents any unauthorized physical access or tampering with the hardware, which could compromise the integrity of the digital evidence. Physical security measures, such as locking down the systems and restricting access, help maintain the original state of the evidence until it can be properly collected and analyzed.

Question 167

During a forensic analysis, you are tasked with examining the integrity of a log file after a suspected breach. What should you primarily look for to ensure the logs have not been tampered with?

- A) Searching for hidden files and unauthorized software installations.
- B) Observing changes in file sizes and timestamps that may indicate unauthorized modifications.
- C) Analyzing user access logs for signs of unauthorized access attempts.
- D) Checking for hash values that match previously generated and securely stored hashes.

Correct Answer: D

Explanation: Hash values are unique to each file or batch of data and are used to verify integrity by comparing the current hash of the file with a previously calculated hash that was stored securely. If the hashes match, it indicates that the file has not been altered since the hash was last calculated, thereby affirming its integrity post-breach.

Question 168

Fill in the blank: In incident response, maintaining _____ of evidence is critical to ensure that findings are admissible in court.

- A) evidence integrity
- B) record of findings
- C) control of access
- D) chain of custody

Correct Answer: D

Explanation: "Chain of custody" refers to the documentation and handling process that records the seizure, custody, control, transfer, analysis, and disposition of evidence. Maintaining a clear chain of custody ensures that the evidence can be legally considered reliable and untampered, supporting its admissibility in court proceedings.

Question 169

An incident responder receives a report that a company server has been compromised. What should be their first action to ensure effective evidence collection?

- A) Isolating the affected system from the network to prevent further contamination.
- B) Conducting a meeting with the IT department to discuss the breach.
- C) Alerting the legal department to potential data breaches that may require compliance actions.
- D) Updating security protocols and installing patches to prevent further breaches.

Correct Answer: A

Explanation: Isolating the affected system is a crucial first step in any forensic investigation of a compromised server as it prevents the potential for further data loss or damage by ensuring that the system cannot be accessed remotely. This isolation helps preserve the state of the system as it was during the compromise, which is vital for a thorough investigation.

Question 170

After discovering unauthorized access to a network, a forensic investigator uses a specific tool to capture volatile memory data. Which tool is best suited for this task?

- A) Using a write-blocking device to prevent data alteration during the capture process.
- B) Applying data recovery techniques to restore any corrupted or deleted files.
- C) Employing antivirus software to scan for and remove malware present in the memory.
- D) Utilizing network monitoring tools to trace the source of the attack in real-time.

Correct Answer: A

Explanation: A write-blocking device is critical in forensic investigations involving volatile memory (e.g., RAM) because it allows the investigator to capture and analyze data in memory without risking alteration of the evidence. This tool ensures that no new data is written to the device, preserving the original state of the digital evidence for analysis.

Question 171

What is the primary purpose of network segmentation in a DLP strategy?

- A) Limiting the scope of potential data exposure and facilitating targeted DLP controls.
- B) Increasing the redundancy of data storage to prevent data loss during network failures.
- C) Reducing the cost of implementing security controls by consolidating network resources.
- D) Enhancing the overall network speed by reducing congestion and improving data flow.

Correct Answer: A

Explanation: Network segmentation as a DLP strategy is fundamental because it confines data flows to specific areas within the network, which limits the spread of any breach and makes it easier to apply stringent DLP controls where they are most needed. This targeted approach not only enhances the protection of sensitive data but also allows for more efficient monitoring and response mechanisms.

Question 172

In the context of DLP, what does the term "content discovery" specifically refer to?

- A) Auditing user activity logs to detect irregular access patterns and potential breaches.
- B) Creating a public awareness campaign about the company's data handling practices.
- C) Identifying the location of sensitive data stored across the organization's digital assets.
- D) Monitoring real-time data transfer rates to identify potential data leaks.

Correct Answer: C

Explanation: Content discovery in DLP involves scanning and identifying locations where sensitive data resides within an organization's digital environments. This process is crucial because it ensures that all potential risk points are known and can be monitored effectively under the DLP policy, thus mitigating the risk of unexpected data leaks from overlooked storage locations.

Question 173

Fill in the blank: To prevent unauthorized data transfers, DLP systems often employ _____ rules based on data types and user actions.

- A) encryption enforcement
- B) metadata tagging
- C) contextual analysis
- D) user role assignment

Correct Answer: C

Explanation: Contextual analysis in DLP refers to the examination of the context in which data is used or moved, allowing for dynamic application of DLP rules based on the content being handled and the actions of the users. This enables the system to differentiate between normal and suspicious activities, adapting its response to prevent unauthorized data transfers effectively.

Question 174

Your company handles sensitive client data and needs a DLP policy to prevent unauthorized data leakage. What is the first step in creating an effective DLP policy?

- A) Identifying what data needs to be protected and categorizing data based on sensitivity.
- B) Purchasing the latest DLP software without assessing company-specific needs.
- C) Training all employees on the basics of cybersecurity and the importance of data protection.
- D) Immediately revising the company's existing security policies to include harsher penalties.

Correct Answer: A

Explanation: The initial step in crafting a DLP policy involves identifying the specific types of data that require protection and understanding their sensitivity levels. This categorization is vital as it determines the security measures that will be implemented, ensuring that highly sensitive data receives the most stringent protection to mitigate the risk of data breaches.

Question 175

An organization plans to implement a new DLP solution to monitor and block sensitive data from being transmitted via email. Which method is most effective?

- A) Implementing endpoint security solutions that restrict user access to sensitive data.
- B) Integrating the DLP system with the existing email server to scan and filter outbound emails.
- C) Conducting regular security audits to ensure compliance with internal data handling policies.
- D) Upgrading physical security measures around data storage locations to prevent theft or tampering.

Correct Answer: B

Explanation: Integrating a DLP solution with an organization's email server to scan and filter outbound emails is highly effective because it directly addresses a common data leakage pathway. This integration allows for real-time scanning of all outgoing communications, ensuring that sensitive information is caught and blocked before it can leave the organization's network, thus preventing potential data breaches.

Question 176

When configuring a next-gen firewall, what is essential for controlling application-level traffic?

- A) Enforcing a policy that blocks all incoming traffic from unknown external sources.
- B) Increasing the firewall's throughput capacity to handle higher traffic volume.
- C) Setting up rules based on the application's signature and behavior.
- D) Reducing the number of open ports to the minimum necessary to reduce vulnerabilities.

Correct Answer: C

Explanation: Configuring rules based on application signatures and behaviors in next-gen firewalls allows for precise control over application-level traffic. This feature enables the firewall to not only block or allow applications but also to enforce policies based on how these applications behave within the network, making it an effective tool for maintaining network security against application-based threats.

Question 177

What feature of next-gen firewalls is critical for protecting against threats hidden in encrypted traffic?

- A) Enabling deep packet inspection to analyze the content of encrypted packets.
- B) Installing a robust antivirus system to scan all incoming and outgoing traffic.
- C) Configuring automatic security updates to ensure the firewall's firmware is current.
- D) Setting the firewall to a default-deny posture for all incoming connections.

Correct Answer: A

Explanation: Deep packet inspection (DPI) of encrypted traffic is crucial as it allows the firewall to examine the contents of encrypted packets without decrypting them. This capability is essential for identifying and mitigating threats that hide within SSL/TLS encrypted traffic, providing an additional layer of security by inspecting data that would otherwise be concealed.

Question 178

Fill in the blank: In configuring next-gen firewalls, setting up ____ inspection is key to defending against modern malware.

- A) resource allocation
- B) load balancing
- C) priority queuing
- D) intrusion detection

Correct Answer: D

Explanation: Intrusion detection systems integrated into next-gen firewalls play a pivotal role in identifying and responding to modern malware threats. These systems analyze network traffic for signs of malicious activities and known threat patterns, enabling proactive defenses against new and evolving security threats.

Question 179

A system administrator is setting up a next-gen firewall for a large organization. What should be prioritized to enhance network security effectively?

- A) Regularly updating firewall rules to reflect changes in internal network structures.
- B) Creating security zones that segment the network based on trust levels and access needs.
- C) Implementing a strict password policy for devices connecting to the network.
- D) Prioritizing high-bandwidth applications to ensure they receive enough resources.

Correct Answer: B

Explanation: Security zones are fundamental in next-gen firewall configuration as they allow the network to be segmented based on varying trust levels and access requirements. By creating these zones, administrators can enforce strict controls on traffic moving between different parts of the network, thereby enhancing security by limiting the potential impact of breaches within low-trust zones.

Question 180

While implementing a next-gen firewall, which configuration is essential to manage and mitigate internal threats?

- A) Deploying additional firewalls at key network entry points for redundant security.
- B) Integrating the firewall with an external threat intelligence service for real-time updates.
- C) Limiting user access to control settings on the firewall to prevent unauthorized changes.
- D) Establishing a system for continuous monitoring of network activity and anomaly detection.

Correct Answer: D

Explanation: Continuous monitoring and anomaly detection within next-gen firewall configurations are vital for managing internal threats. This system enables real-time detection of unusual network behaviors that could indicate internal security threats or policy violations, allowing for immediate investigation and response to potential risks.

Question 181

What is the primary function of a Network Access Control (NAC) system in a corporate environment?

- A) To increase the overall bandwidth available to authenticated users by restricting access to unauthorized users.
- B) To monitor and log the web activity of devices connected to the network for behavioral analysis.
- C) To provide uninterrupted power supplies to critical network components to ensure availability.
- D) To authenticate and authorize devices based on compliance with security policies before allowing network access.

Correct Answer: D

Explanation: The primary function of a Network Access Control (NAC) system is to ensure that all devices connected to the network are authenticated and authorized based on predefined security policies. This process prevents unauthorized access and ensures that only compliant devices can connect to and interact with network resources, thus safeguarding the corporate environment from potential security threats.

Question 182

How does a NAC system enforce security policies on devices attempting to access network resources?

- A) Requiring two-factor authentication for all devices, regardless of their security compliance status.
- B) By assessing the security posture of devices before granting them access to the network.
- C) Implementing bandwidth limitations on devices that do not meet the required security standards.
- D) Using artificial intelligence to predict which devices might become non-compliant in the future.

Correct Answer: B

Explanation: A NAC system enforces security policies by initially assessing the security posture of any device attempting to access network resources. This assessment typically involves checking the device's configuration, software updates, and security features against the organization's standards. If a device does not meet these standards, it can be denied access, thus preventing potential security risks.

Question 183

Fill in the blank: To enhance network security, NAC systems often integrate with _____ management systems to assess device compliance before granting access.

- A) identity
- B) inventory
- C) patch
- D) performance

Correct Answer: C

Explanation: Patch management integration is essential for NAC systems because it allows the system to verify that all devices attempting to connect to the network are up-to-date with the latest security patches. This integration helps in preventing access by devices that could be vulnerable to known threats and exploits, thereby enhancing the overall security of the network.

Question 184

When implementing a NAC solution, a network administrator must ensure secure access for remote workers. What is the best practice?

- A) Creating a dedicated network segment for remote workers that is isolated from the core network.
- B) Allowing remote workers to bypass NAC requirements to maintain productivity and ease of access.
- C) Using a virtual private network (VPN) in conjunction with NAC to secure remote connections.
- D) Deploying additional firewall software on devices used by remote workers to enhance security.

Correct Answer: C

Explanation: Implementing a VPN in conjunction with NAC solutions is a best practice for securing remote access. This combination ensures that all data transmitted between the remote worker's device and the network is encrypted and that the device is assessed for compliance before it can access network resources, thus extending secure access control to remote environments.

Question 185

During an audit, it was found that unauthorized devices were accessing the network. Which NAC feature should be enhanced to prevent such incidents?

- A) Increasing the frequency of security audits to identify and address network access violations.
- B) Upgrading the physical security measures at network access points to prevent physical tampering.
- C) Implementing stronger encryption methods on data transmitted over the network.
- D) Strengthening the endpoint compliance checks to verify device configurations against company policies.

Correct Answer: D

Explanation: Strengthening endpoint compliance checks within a NAC framework involves rigorously verifying that each device conforms to the organization's security configurations and policies before it is allowed network access. Enhancing this feature helps in catching any unauthorized or non-compliant devices before they can access sensitive network areas, effectively mitigating the risk of security breaches.

Question 186

What is the primary goal of integrating security practices within the DevOps lifecycle?

- A) To streamline regulatory compliance by automating documentation processes.
- B) To reduce the cost of software deployment by minimizing the need for post-production patches.
- C) To increase the speed of development cycles by eliminating the need for a dedicated security team.
- D) To detect and resolve security issues early, reducing the risk of vulnerabilities in

production.

Correct Answer: D

Explanation: Integrating security practices within the DevOps lifecycle aims to identify and address security issues at the earliest possible stage. This approach significantly reduces the risk of vulnerabilities reaching production environments, as potential security problems are resolved before deployment. This proactive stance not only enhances the security of the software but also minimizes costly and time-consuming remediation efforts after release.

Question 187

During the initial phase of a DevSecOps project, what is critical to establishing a secure foundation?

- A) Launching a comprehensive training program for developers on secure coding practices.
- B) Prioritizing the deployment of the most advanced security tools available.
- C) Conducting a thorough risk assessment to identify and prioritize security needs.
- D) Assigning a security champion within the team who has basic security training.

Correct Answer: C

Explanation: Conducting a thorough risk assessment at the beginning of a DevSecOps project is critical as it helps identify potential security threats and vulnerabilities that could impact the project. By understanding and prioritizing these risks, the team can implement targeted security measures from the start, effectively laying a secure foundation for the development lifecycle.

Question 188

Fill in the blank: Continuous _____ is essential for detecting vulnerabilities early in the DevSecOps cycle.

- A) deployment
- B) monitoring
- C) documentation
- D) integration

Correct Answer: D

Explanation: Continuous integration in DevSecOps environments involves regularly merging code changes into a central repository, followed by automated building and testing. This practice is essential for detecting vulnerabilities early in the development cycle because it ensures that every change is immediately tested, allowing for quick identification and remediation of security issues.

Question 189

A DevOps team is preparing to launch a new service. What step should be prioritized to ensure the security and reliability of the service from the outset?

- A) Implementing automated security testing tools in the CI/CD pipeline.
- B) Initiating public bug bounty programs early to catch any security flaws.
- C) Enhancing collaboration between development and operations teams without a security focus.
- D) Focusing on rapid deployment strategies to outpace potential cyber threats.

Correct Answer: A

Explanation: Implementing automated security testing tools within the Continuous Integration/Continuous Deployment (CI/CD) pipeline is a key step for ensuring the security and reliability of new services. These tools automatically scan for vulnerabilities as part of the deployment process, providing immediate feedback on the security posture of the software at every change, thereby maintaining a high security standard throughout the development lifecycle.

Question 190

In a DevSecOps environment, which practice is most effective for preventing security vulnerabilities in production code?

- A) Relying on penetration testing conducted by external consultants at project milestones.
- B) Scheduling regular manual code reviews at the end of each development sprint.
- C) Incorporating automated code reviews with static code analysis tools.
- D) Developing an in-house security protocol that is reviewed quarterly by the IT department.

Correct Answer: C

Explanation: Incorporating automated code reviews using static code analysis tools is highly effective in a DevSecOps environment as it allows for the automatic detection of security flaws within the codebase. These tools analyze the code for known vulnerability patterns and provide feedback without requiring manual code reviews, thus enhancing the efficiency and security of the development process. This automated approach ensures that security considerations are seamlessly integrated into the development workflow, significantly reducing the likelihood of security vulnerabilities making it to production.

Question 191

What is the main goal of using behavioral analytics in cybersecurity systems?

- A) Enhancing the efficiency of system resources by automatically adjusting security settings.
- B) Identifying unusual activities in user behavior that may indicate a security breach.
- C) Improving system performance by detecting and stopping resource-intensive processes.
- D) Logging and analyzing all network traffic to identify potential bandwidth bottlenecks.

Correct Answer: B

Explanation: The main goal of using behavioral analytics in cybersecurity is to identify activities that deviate from normal user behavior, which could indicate a potential security breach. By focusing on behavior rather than specific threats, behavioral analytics can detect new and evolving threats that traditional signature-based systems might miss.

Question 192

How does a behavioral analytics system detect abnormal patterns in a network environment?

- A) Tracking network traffic spikes to ensure bandwidth is available for critical operations.
- B) By analyzing user and system activity to establish a baseline and detect deviations from it.
- C) Identifying high-bandwidth users to ensure fair distribution of network resources.
- D) Generating reports on system resource usage to optimize performance and prevent overload.

Correct Answer: B

Explanation: Behavioral analytics systems function by creating a baseline of normal activity for users and systems. Once this baseline is established, any deviation from these typical patterns is flagged as potentially suspicious. This method allows the system to detect anomalies that could indicate malicious activity, such as unauthorized access or data theft.

Question 193

Fill in the blank: Behavioral analytics helps identify security threats by comparing current activity to _____ behavior.

- A) traffic patterns
- B) historical logs

- C) user credentials
- D) baseline

Correct Answer: D

Explanation: Behavioral analytics relies on establishing a "baseline" of normal activity for users and systems, allowing the system to compare current actions against this baseline. When the current activity deviates from the baseline, it triggers an alert or further investigation, helping to catch suspicious behaviors that may go unnoticed in static rule-based systems.

Question 194

A system administrator notices a user account accessing large amounts of data at unusual hours. How should a behavioral analytics tool respond to this situation?

- A) Automatically terminating the user session without further investigation to prevent data exfiltration.
- B) Ignoring the activity if no immediate malware is detected in the accessed data.
- C) Flagging the activity for investigation as it deviates from typical user behavior patterns.
- D) Sending a general alert to all users to notify them of potential security risks.

Correct Answer: C

Explanation: In cases where a behavioral analytics tool detects unusual access patterns, such as a user account accessing large amounts of data at odd hours, the system should flag the activity for investigation. Since it deviates from typical behavior, it may indicate unauthorized access or malicious intent, requiring further analysis to confirm whether it's a threat.

Question 195

While monitoring a corporate network, an analyst discovers an employee's workstation downloading unauthorized software. What is the best approach for a behavioral analytics system to handle this scenario?

- A) Allowing the software to run if it passes antivirus scans and no malware is detected.
- B) Shutting down the network connection for all employees to prevent further security issues.
- C) Automatically disconnecting the workstation from the network without further analysis.
- D) Automatically raising an alert and blocking the suspicious activity based on established behavioral norms.

Correct Answer: D

Explanation: When behavioral analytics systems detect a workstation downloading unauthorized software, they should raise an alert and block the activity, as it violates the normal behavioral patterns of the employee and could indicate a compromised system. This proactive approach helps to prevent potential security incidents while ensuring that anomalous behavior is handled immediately.

Question 196

How do email security gateways prevent phishing attacks in an enterprise environment?

- A) By performing regular password changes for email accounts and limiting access based on device security levels.
- B) By blocking emails based on sender reputation, regardless of the message content.
- C) By filtering incoming emails for known malicious URLs and attachments based on threat intelligence databases.
- D) By forcing users to authenticate their email addresses before sending messages to the internal network.

Correct Answer: C

Explanation: Email security gateways use threat intelligence databases to filter incoming emails for malicious URLs and attachments. By cross-referencing emails with known phishing and malware indicators, the gateway can prevent phishing emails from reaching users. This proactive filtering method effectively blocks malicious content before it poses a risk to the organization.

Question 197

What method is most effective for an email security gateway to detect and block malware attachments?

- A) By increasing the spam filter strength to minimize the number of emails reaching the recipient inbox.
- B) By setting a size limit on attachments to prevent the delivery of large files that could contain malware.
- C) By disabling attachments entirely, preventing any files from being transmitted through email.
- D) By scanning attachments in real-time using signature-based and heuristic detection techniques.

Correct Answer: D

Explanation: Scanning attachments in real-time using signature-based and heuristic techniques is crucial for detecting malware. Signature-based scanning identifies known malware by comparing the file to a database of known malware signatures, while heuristic techniques analyze the behavior and structure of the attachment to detect previously unknown malware. This combination ensures that both known and emerging threats are detected and blocked.

Question 198

Fill in the blank: To reduce the risk of phishing, email security gateways use _____ filtering to analyze message headers and contents.

- A) subject

- B) header
- C) content
- D) signature

Correct Answer: C

Explanation: Content filtering is employed by email security gateways to analyze the body of the email and its metadata for suspicious elements, such as malicious links, attachments, or phishing-related phrases. By focusing on the message content and headers, the gateway can detect phishing attempts that may otherwise bypass basic security measures.

Question 199

A security administrator notices a sudden increase in phishing emails bypassing the gateway. What step should they take to improve protection?

- A) Restricting the use of external email providers and enforcing strict sender authentication.
- B) Isolating all email communications to an internal network and disallowing external emails.
- C) Updating the gateway's phishing detection algorithms and enabling advanced machine learning models.
- D) Increasing the frequency of user security awareness training sessions to recognize phishing attempts.

Correct Answer: C

Explanation: When phishing emails bypass an email security gateway, it is often due to outdated detection algorithms. By updating the gateway's phishing detection algorithms and incorporating advanced machine learning models, the gateway can improve its ability to recognize and block phishing attempts more effectively. Machine learning enhances the gateway's ability to adapt to new phishing tactics that evolve over time.

Question 200

A company is concerned about malware hidden in attachments sent through email. Which feature should the email security gateway prioritize to mitigate this risk?

- A) Deploying enhanced antivirus scanning on the gateway to detect embedded malware.
- B) Enabling sandboxing to execute attachments in a secure environment before delivery.
- C) Setting a policy to delete all attachments that are not from trusted contacts or domains.
- D) Limiting the types of attachments allowed through the gateway to minimize risks.

Correct Answer: B

Explanation: Sandboxing is a highly effective feature for email security gateways as it allows suspicious attachments to be executed in a controlled environment before being delivered to the recipient. This process helps identify hidden malware by observing how the attachment behaves in a safe environment, ensuring that any malicious content is detected and blocked without putting the network at risk.

Question 201

Which of the following activities best demonstrates how an ethical hacker can assist an organization in aligning its security strategy with its business goals?

- A) Randomly testing security systems without any strategic planning or alignment with business objectives.
- B) Developing a generic set of security policies that apply to all departments regardless of their specific functions.
- C) Conducting a risk assessment specific to the business sector to tailor the cybersecurity framework effectively.
- D) Training the cybersecurity team on the latest hacking techniques without considering business-specific threats.

Correct Answer: C

Explanation: By conducting a risk assessment that is specifically tailored to the business sector, an ethical hacker can identify unique threats and vulnerabilities that directly impact the organization's strategic goals, allowing for the development of a more effective cybersecurity framework that supports these objectives.

Question 202

Fill in the blank: To ensure security practices align with business goals, it is essential for an ethical hacker to understand the organization's _____.

- A) Competitive advantage
- B) Revenue streams
- C) Business model
- D) Strategic plan

Correct Answer: C

Explanation: Understanding the business model is crucial for ethical hackers as it helps them identify critical assets and processes that need protection, align security measures with business objectives, and prioritize security tasks based on business needs, ensuring that security enhancements directly support business functionality.

Question 203

A company plans to expand its operations into e-commerce, which requires enhanced security measures. As an ethical hacker, what should be the first step in aligning the security strategy with this new business goal?

- A) Upgrading all company hardware to the latest models to enhance overall security.
- B) Conducting a threat modeling session to identify potential security threats specific to e-commerce.
- C) Drafting an email to all employees about general security best practices.
- D) Recommending the use of standard antivirus software across all new online platforms.

Correct Answer: B

Explanation: Threat modeling for an e-commerce expansion helps in identifying and mitigating potential threats early in the deployment phase. This proactive approach ensures that the security strategy is aligned with business goals by protecting against threats specific to e-commerce activities, which can include transaction fraud or data breaches, thereby supporting the business's expansion goals safely.

Question 204

During a routine assessment, an ethical hacker finds that the current security measures do not align with the organization's growth targets. What is the most appropriate recommendation to make?

- A) Advise against any changes as it might disrupt the current operational workflow.
- B) Recommend updating the risk management framework to include specific controls that address future scalability and integration needs.
- C) Proposing a decrease in security budget since the targets involve only moderate growth.
- D) Suggest maintaining the current security posture as the company has not yet encountered any significant security breaches.

Correct Answer: B

Explanation: Updating the risk management framework to address scalability and integration for future growth ensures that the security infrastructure evolves in line with the organization's objectives. This alignment is crucial for supporting long-term growth targets without compromising security, thus fostering a secure yet flexible environment for expansion.

Question 205

An ethical hacker is tasked with reviewing a company's new mobile application that will handle sensitive customer data. What is a critical action to ensure security measures align with business objectives?

- A) Only conducting performance testing to ensure the application can handle high user volumes.
- B) Implement continuous security monitoring and integrate it with the company's incident response plan.
- C) Focusing solely on the encryption of data stored within the application.
- D) Suggesting a one-time security audit to evaluate the application's compliance with industry standards.

Correct Answer: B

Explanation: Implementing continuous security monitoring and integrating it with the incident response plan ensures that security measures evolve with the new business initiatives, like the launch of a sensitive mobile application. This alignment helps in quickly identifying and mitigating any security incidents that could impact the business objectives, thus maintaining customer trust and compliance with regulatory requirements.

Question 206

What is the first step in developing a security program roadmap that aligns with both short-term and long-term organizational objectives?

- A) Drafting an immediate action plan to address any perceived threats without further analysis.
- B) Establishing a broad set of goals that are not directly tied to specific business objectives.
- C) Creating a detailed list of all software and hardware assets without prioritizing them.
- D) Identifying key business drivers and current security posture through assessments.

Correct Answer: D

Explanation: The initial step of identifying key business drivers and evaluating the current security posture allows an ethical hacker to create a foundational understanding of where the organization stands and where it needs to go. This tailored assessment ensures that the roadmap is realistically aligned with both immediate security needs and long-term business goals, making it effective and strategic.

Question 207

Fill in the blank: In the context of a security program roadmap, it is crucial for ethical hackers to prioritize tasks that safeguard the company's _____.

- A) Critical infrastructure
- B) Most used applications
- C) Software development practices
- D) Employee data

Correct Answer: A

Explanation: Prioritizing the protection of critical infrastructure within the security program roadmap is essential as it encompasses the most vital assets that, if compromised, could cause significant operational disruption or financial loss. This focus ensures the organization's resilience against attacks that could severely impact its core functions.

Question 208

In creating a security roadmap, which element should an ethical hacker focus on to ensure alignment with the organization's future growth and evolving threat landscape?

- A) Adopting the latest cybersecurity trends irrespective of their alignment with the company's needs.
- B) Integrating regular security assessments to adapt to changes and identify new vulnerabilities.
- C) Recommending the use of a single security framework for all types of company operations.
- D) Focusing solely on current technologies without planning for future updates or threats.

Correct Answer: B

Explanation: Integrating regular security assessments within the roadmap allows for continual adaptation to new and evolving threats as well as changes within the organization itself, such as expansions or technological upgrades. This proactive approach helps maintain security alignment with the organization's growth trajectory and the dynamic nature of cyber threats.

Question 209

A company is integrating new IoT devices across its network. What should be the primary focus for an ethical hacker when updating the security program roadmap?

- A) Implementing the strongest possible encryption methods immediately on all devices.
- B) Focusing exclusively on cost-cutting measures in security budgeting.
- C) Limiting the roadmap to existing network infrastructure without considering IoT integrations.
- D) Ensuring that security controls are scalable and adaptable to new technologies and threats.

Correct Answer: D

Explanation: When integrating IoT devices, it is vital to ensure that the updated security program roadmap includes scalable and adaptable controls. This focus on flexibility helps in accommodating not only the current but also future technological advancements and emerging threats, thus maintaining robust security amid evolving infrastructural changes.

Question 210

An ethical hacker is tasked with developing a security program roadmap for a financial institution facing increased cyber threats. What should be the key consideration?

- A) Focusing on international compliance standards regardless of specific threats to the organization.
- B) Emphasizing employee training over technological defenses and threat assessments.

- C) Prioritizing the protection of customer data and transaction security systems.
- D) Concentrating solely on perimeter defenses like firewalls and antivirus systems.

Correct Answer: C

Explanation: For a financial institution, prioritizing the protection of customer data and transaction systems within the security program roadmap addresses the most critical assets from a risk and compliance perspective. This focus is paramount in maintaining trust, safeguarding against financial fraud, and complying with stringent regulatory requirements that govern financial data security.

Question 211

What is the most critical factor to consider when budgeting for a security program to ensure resources are allocated effectively?

- A) The preferences of the security team, focusing on the technologies they are most familiar with.
- B) The amount of funding received in the previous fiscal year without considering current needs.
- C) The latest cybersecurity trends, regardless of their direct impact on the organization's core assets.
- D) The alignment of security initiatives with the organization's strategic objectives.

Correct Answer: D

Explanation: When budgeting for a security program, aligning security initiatives with organizational strategic objectives ensures that the allocated resources directly support the broader goals of the company. This alignment helps in prioritizing spending on areas that will provide the most significant benefit in terms of risk mitigation and strategic value, thereby optimizing the use of available funds.

Question 212

Fill in the blank: When planning the budget for a security program, it is essential to assess the _____ to determine resource allocation priorities.

- A) Risk landscape
- B) Historical spending
- C) Employee satisfaction
- D) Number of IT staff

Correct Answer: A

Explanation: Understanding the risk landscape is essential for effective budgeting in security programs because it helps identify where threats are most likely to impact the organization. This assessment allows for targeted resource allocation to areas with higher risks, ensuring that spending is both strategic and justified, which maximizes the impact of the security budget.

Question 213

A company is planning to expand its security operations to include advanced threat detection systems. How should the budget be adjusted?

- A) Redirect all unused funds from the previous year to cover the costs without additional adjustments.
- B) Cut costs in other less critical areas to fund the new systems without increasing the total budget.
- C) Increase the budget proportionally to cover both initial capital expenses and ongoing operational costs.
- D) Assume that existing budgets are sufficient and request additional funding only if a shortfall occurs.

Correct Answer: C

Explanation: For the inclusion of advanced threat detection systems, it is crucial to budget not only for the initial setup costs but also for ongoing operational expenses. This comprehensive budgeting ensures that the systems are effectively supported over time, maintaining their functionality and ensuring they provide sustained value to the security operations.

Question 214

During a budget review, it's noted that the current allocation does not cover new regulatory compliance costs. What should be the immediate focus?

- A) Maintain the current budget distribution, assuming compliance costs can be absorbed by efficiencies elsewhere.
- B) Adjust the budget to prioritize new compliance technologies and necessary training programs.
- C) Suggest reducing the scope of regulatory requirements to avoid additional expenses.
- D) Delay addressing compliance costs, focusing on other areas deemed more critical by the security team.

Correct Answer: B

Explanation: When new regulatory compliance costs arise, it is important to adjust the security budget to cover the expenses associated with implementing compliant technologies and staff training programs. This prioritization ensures that the organization can meet legal requirements, thereby avoiding potential fines and enhancing the overall security posture.

Question 215

An organization is reallocating its security budget in response to a recent data breach. What should be prioritized to prevent future incidents?

- A) Allocate additional funds to incident response capabilities and advanced forensic tools.
- B) Focus spending on upgrading all outdated software and hardware systems.
- C) Concentrate on public relations efforts to restore reputation rather than on enhancing security measures.
- D) Invest primarily in physical security enhancements, such as access controls and surveillance.

Correct Answer: A

Explanation: Following a data breach, prioritizing incident response capabilities and advanced forensic tools in the budget is crucial. This allocation helps strengthen the organization's ability to respond effectively to incidents and to investigate breaches thoroughly, which is key to preventing future security issues and minimizing the impact of similar events.

Question 216

What is a fundamental requirement when managing security vendor relationships to ensure data protection?

- A) Trusting vendor assurances of security without requesting detailed security documentation or evidence.
- B) Allowing vendors to self-certify their compliance without conducting any independent verification.
- C) Focusing solely on the cost-effectiveness of the vendor's services without evaluating their security standards.
- D) Ensuring all vendors comply with organizational security policies and regulations.

Correct Answer: D

Explanation: Ensuring that all security vendors comply with the organization's own security policies and regulatory requirements is crucial. This alignment helps to maintain a consistent security posture across all external engagements and protects the organization from potential vulnerabilities introduced by external parties.

Question 217

Fill in the blank: Regular _____ with security vendors ensures alignment with security protocols and contractual obligations.

- A) Reviews and audits
- B) Team-building events
- C) Feedback sessions
- D) Annual celebrations

Correct Answer: A

Explanation: Regular reviews and audits with security vendors are essential to ensure that they continually meet the security requirements specified in their contracts. This ongoing scrutiny helps in early identification of discrepancies and allows for timely corrective actions, ensuring that security standards are consistently upheld.

Question 218

During a security audit, it's discovered that a vendor is not complying with contractual security requirements. What should be the initial response?

- A) Initiate a formal compliance review and re-evaluate the vendor's contract and performance.
- B) Immediately terminate the contract without investigating the reasons behind the non-compliance.
- C) Offer additional training to the vendor's staff in an informal setup to encourage better compliance.
- D) Ignore the findings as long as there are no actual security breaches reported.

Correct Answer: A

Explanation: Initiating a formal compliance review is the appropriate first step when a vendor fails to meet contractual security obligations. This process should re-evaluate the vendor's performance and adherence to the contract, providing a systematic approach to address and rectify issues, thereby maintaining the integrity of the security framework.

Question 219

When selecting a new security vendor, what is the most important factor to consider to maintain compliance with industry standards?

- A) Assessing the vendor's certifications and adherence to relevant security standards.
- B) Focusing on the vendor's location as the critical factor due to data sovereignty concerns.
- C) Evaluating only the technological aspects of the vendor's offerings without considering their security practices.
- D) Choosing a vendor based primarily on their market popularity and brand recognition.

Correct Answer: A

Explanation: Assessing a vendor's certifications and their adherence to relevant security standards is vital during the selection process. This evaluation ensures that the vendor follows industry best practices and meets compliance requirements, which is crucial for maintaining the security and integrity of the organization's data and systems.

Question 220

An organization is reviewing its security vendor contracts. What should be prioritized to enhance security management?

- A) Limiting the scope of the security reviews to digital assets only, excluding physical security.
- B) Updating contract terms to include regular security audits and penalty clauses for non-compliance.
- C) Emphasizing flexibility in contract terms to accommodate future technological changes.
- D) Prioritizing the reduction of contract costs over specifying security performance metrics.

Correct Answer: B

Explanation: Updating security vendor contracts to include regular security audits and enforce penalty clauses for non-compliance is critical. These provisions ensure that vendors remain vigilant about their security obligations and that there are clear consequences for failing to meet these standards, which ultimately enhances overall security management.

Question 221

What is a critical first step in conducting a vendor risk assessment?

- A) Starting with an assessment of the vendor's corporate culture and alignment with the company.
- B) Conducting random spot-checks on the vendor's operations without a structured assessment plan.
- C) Checking the financial stability of the vendor without considering their security posture.
- D) Identifying and classifying all data that the vendor will access or store.

Correct Answer: D

Explanation: Identifying and classifying all data the vendor will access or store is critical as it sets the scope for the risk assessment. This initial step ensures that the assessment can accurately evaluate how vendor interactions might expose the organization to risks, particularly concerning data security and compliance requirements.

Question 222

Fill in the blank: Comprehensive vendor risk assessments require detailed knowledge of the vendor's _____.

- A) Security policies and data handling procedures
- B) Marketing strategies
- C) Customer service ratings
- D) Organizational structure

Correct Answer: A

Explanation: Understanding the vendor's security policies and their data handling procedures is essential to determine how well the vendor can protect sensitive information. This knowledge helps assess the risk level associated with the vendor and whether additional controls are necessary to mitigate potential security gaps.

Question 223

When evaluating a new software provider, what key aspect should be included in the risk assessment?

- A) Focusing on user interface design features of the software over its security protocols.
- B) Ensuring the software is compatible with existing systems, disregarding security implications.
- C) Evaluating the software provider's data encryption standards and compliance with industry regulations.
- D) Reviewing only the cost-effectiveness of the software without assessing security features.

Correct Answer: C

Explanation: Evaluating a software provider's data encryption standards and compliance with relevant industry regulations is crucial. These factors directly impact the security of the software and, by extension, the security of the organization's data, making this aspect a vital part of the risk assessment process.

Question 224

A company is reassessing the risks associated with its long-time hardware supplier due to new regulatory changes. What is an essential factor to consider?

- A) Focusing solely on the price of the hardware without considering its compliance with new regulations.
- B) Assessing the impact of regulatory changes on the supplier's ability to meet security requirements.
- C) Evaluating the potential for reduced delivery times that might result from the new regulations.
- D) Assessing how the hardware supplier's location might affect shipping costs under new regulations.

Correct Answer: B

Explanation: When regulatory changes occur, assessing their impact on a supplier's ability to meet security requirements is essential. This ensures that the supplier remains compliant with both new and existing regulations, which is crucial for maintaining the integrity and security of the supply chain.

Question 225

During contract negotiations with a cloud service provider, what should be prioritized in the risk assessment?

- A) Considering only the scalability of services offered by the cloud provider.
- B) Prioritizing the geographic location of the cloud provider's data centers above all else.
- C) Focusing on immediate cost savings offered by the cloud service without assessing long-term risks.
- D) Examining the cloud provider's data breach history and recovery capabilities.

Correct Answer: D

Explanation: Examining a cloud provider's history of data breaches and their recovery capabilities is vital in a risk assessment. This analysis helps gauge the provider's resilience and reliability, which are critical factors in maintaining data integrity and availability in cloud-based operations.

Question 226

What should be included at the start of the procurement process to ensure security considerations are integrated?

- A) A security requirements checklist aligned with organizational security policies.
- B) An initial cost analysis to determine the financial impact of security measures on the procurement.
- C) Setting a flexible timeline for procurement to adjust for security vetting as needed.
- D) A broad statement of work that does not specify security requirements but expects compliance.

Correct Answer: A

Explanation: Including a security requirements checklist at the start of the procurement process ensures that all potential vendors are aware of the security standards they must meet. This checklist helps align vendor offerings with the organization's security policies from the outset, thereby facilitating a security-focused procurement process.

Question 227

Fill in the blank: It is crucial to incorporate security reviews during the _____ stage of the procurement lifecycle to identify potential risks.

- A) Final payment
- B) Contract signing
- C) Vendor selection
- D) Initial inquiry

Correct Answer: C

Explanation: Incorporating security reviews during the vendor selection stage is critical for identifying potential risks early in the procurement lifecycle. This step ensures that vendors' security practices are scrutinized before any commitment is made, which is vital for maintaining the organization's security integrity.

Question 228

How should the procurement team respond when a vendor fails to meet the established security requirements during the bidding process?

- A) Choose the lowest bid offering despite the security shortcomings to stay within budget.
- B) Proceed with the vendor who marginally meets the security requirements but offers the best price.
- C) Reopen the bidding process to include a requirement for all vendors to comply with the security criteria.
- D) Implement the vendor's solution on a trial basis to assess security performance before committing.

Correct Answer: C

Explanation: Reopening the bidding process to enforce security compliance ensures that all potential vendors meet the required security standards. This approach not only maintains the integrity of the security posture but also promotes a competitive environment where vendors must prioritize security to be considered.

Question 229

A company is evaluating multiple vendors for a new IT system. What is the key security action before finalizing the procurement?

- A) Select the vendor offering the quickest implementation timeline to speed up deployment.
- B) Prioritize vendors based on their geographic proximity to reduce logistical challenges.
- C) Base the final decision solely on vendor presentations and provided documentation.
- D) Conduct a comprehensive security audit of the proposed solutions from each vendor.

Correct Answer: D

Explanation: Conducting a comprehensive security audit of proposed solutions from different vendors allows the procurement team to evaluate how well each solution meets the required security standards. This critical assessment ensures that the final decision supports the organization's security needs and strategic goals.

Question 230

In revising the procurement policies, what aspect is most important to enhance security measures?

- A) Emphasize the integration of innovative technologies without a focus on their security implications.
- B) Focus solely on speeding up the procurement process to reduce time-to-market for new products.
- C) Ensure the procurement process is transparent to all stakeholders but exclude specific security details.
- D) Mandating that all procurements include a thorough security risk assessment report.

Correct Answer: D

Explanation: Mandating that all procurement actions include a thorough security risk assessment ensures that security considerations are integral to the procurement policies. This requirement helps prevent the introduction of new vulnerabilities through procured products or services and strengthens the overall security framework of the organization.

Question 231

What is a primary consideration when performing a cost-benefit analysis for a new security initiative?

- A) Estimating the potential financial impact of a security breach if the initiative is not implemented.

- B) Determining the preferences of the security team for certain types of security technologies.
- C) Selection based on the quickest implementation time to show immediate results.
- D) Focusing on the least expensive options available regardless of their effectiveness.

Correct Answer: A

Explanation: Estimating the potential financial impact of a security breach is crucial in a cost-benefit analysis for new security initiatives. This estimation helps in understanding the value of investing in security measures by comparing the costs of implementation against the potential losses that could be incurred from security failures, thereby justifying the expenditure.

Question 232

Fill in the blank: A cost-benefit analysis for security projects often requires a detailed review of potential _____ savings from avoiding breaches.

- A) Personnel
- B) Environmental
- C) Hardware
- D) Operational

Correct Answer: D

Explanation: Considering operational savings from avoiding breaches is vital as it quantifies how much the organization can save in terms of reduced downtime, preserved brand reputation, and avoidance of regulatory fines. This helps in making a financially informed decision about the security investments.

Question 233

In a proposal for upgrading cybersecurity tools, what financial aspect must be analyzed to justify the investment?

- A) The vendor's financing options for spreading out the payment over several years.
- B) Immediate costs of implementation without considering future savings or benefits.
- C) Long-term cost reductions in incident response and maintenance compared to initial expenses.
- D) The impact on the company's stock price following the announcement of the upgrade.

Correct Answer: C

Explanation: Analyzing long-term cost reductions in incident response and maintenance against initial expenses is essential in justifying investments in cybersecurity tools. This perspective ensures that the financial benefits of the investment are realized over time, surpassing the upfront costs and sustaining the organization's security posture effectively.

Question 234

An organization considers implementing an advanced intrusion detection system. What is essential to include in the cost-benefit analysis?

- A) Evaluating only the system's features without considering how they reduce risks.
- B) Analysis of the technical compatibility of the new system with existing infrastructure.
- C) Consideration of the vendor's promotional offers as a primary financial benefit.
- D) Estimation of the reduction in potential financial losses from security incidents.

Correct Answer: D

Explanation: Including an estimation of the reduction in potential financial losses from security incidents in the cost-benefit analysis of an advanced intrusion detection system is important. This calculation highlights how the system can mitigate risks and reduce the financial impact of potential breaches, supporting the financial feasibility of the initiative.

Question 235

The company plans to replace its legacy system with a cloud-based security solution. What factor is crucial in the cost-benefit analysis?

- A) Comparison of long-term operational savings against the upfront transition costs.
- B) Prioritizing the user-friendliness of the new system to enhance employee satisfaction.
- C) Emphasis solely on the technological advantages of cloud security without financial considerations.
- D) Assessment of the cloud provider's market reputation and brand strength.

Correct Answer: A

Explanation: Comparing long-term operational savings against upfront transition costs is crucial when considering a shift to a cloud-based security solution. This comparison helps determine if the long-term benefits of reduced operational costs and improved security outweigh the initial investment, facilitating a well-rounded financial decision.

Question 236

What is a crucial factor to consider when determining the appropriate level of security service to outsource?

- A) Specific technologies used by the service provider.
- B) The potential impact of a security breach on the company's operations.
- C) The cost of the service compared to in-house provisioning.
- D) The geographical location of the outsourcing provider.

Correct Answer: B

Explanation: Considering the potential impact of a security breach is vital as it directly relates to the critical assets and functions of the company that could be compromised. This assessment helps in aligning the level of security measures with the specific risks identified.

Question 237

Fill in the blank: When negotiating contracts for outsourcing security services, it's essential to include _____ to ensure compliance and accountability.

- A) Requirements for the provider to hold specific security certifications.
- B) Detailed performance metrics and breach penalties.
- C) Clauses regarding the termination of the service.
- D) Regular update meetings scheduled quarterly.

Correct Answer: B

Explanation: Including detailed performance metrics and breach penalties in contracts ensures that the outsourced provider is held to a high standard of performance and accountability, reducing risks related to non-compliance and underperformance.

Question 238

During a security audit, which element would indicate a well-managed outsourced security service?

- A) Evidence of regular, transparent communication between your company and the service provider.
- B) Provider's compliance with international security standards.
- C) Inconsistencies between reported issues and actual logs.
- D) A low rate of incident reports which may suggest under-reporting.

Correct Answer: A

Explanation: Regular and transparent communication is indicative of a well-managed outsourced security service. It helps in maintaining oversight, ensuring that security measures are correctly implemented, and that any issues are promptly addressed.

Question 239

Which of these would be a red flag in managing outsourced security contracts effectively?

- A) Vague terms concerning the scope of work and responsibilities.
- B) Frequent turnover of the provider's security personnel.
- C) High costs associated with service customization.
- D) Presence of hidden fees in the contract.

Correct Answer: A

Explanation: Vague terms in the contract can lead to misinterpretations and disputes regarding responsibilities and deliverables, which can compromise the security of the organization. Clear, well-defined terms are essential for effective contract management.

Question 240

When transitioning security services to an outsourcing company, what is a critical step to ensure seamless integration and control?

- A) A comprehensive audit of the provider's security practices and past performance.
- B) Conducting a pilot project to test the provider's effectiveness before full implementation.
- C) Implementation of a transitional period with overlap of in-house and outsourced services.
- D) Establishing a joint governance framework with clear roles and responsibilities.

Correct Answer: D

Explanation: Establishing a joint governance framework with clear roles and responsibilities ensures that both the outsourcing provider and the hiring company maintain control and oversight throughout the contract duration, facilitating better coordination and security management.

Question 241
What is the primary purpose of conducting an in-depth background check on a potential vendor?

- A) The geographical location and infrastructure of the vendor.
- B) How quickly the vendor can implement new technologies.
- C) The diversity of services and solutions the vendor offers.
- D) To identify any past legal or financial issues that could affect your business relationship.

Correct Answer: D

Explanation: Conducting in-depth background checks on potential vendors is crucial to uncover any historical legal or financial issues. These issues could potentially compromise the vendor's reliability and negatively impact your business operations by creating risks of non-compliance or financial instability.

Question 242
Fill in the blank: It is critical to verify the vendor's _____ to ensure they can uphold data protection laws relevant to your business.

- A) Compliance history with industry-specific regulations.
- B) Average response time to service disruptions or issues.
- C) Types of data encryption methods they use during data transmission.
- D) The number of years the vendor has been in business.

Correct Answer: A

Explanation: Verifying a vendor's compliance history with industry-specific regulations is essential because it demonstrates their capability to adhere to critical legal standards that protect both the vendor and client against potential legal challenges.

Question 243

In evaluating a vendor's suitability, what must be assessed regarding their past performance?

- A) Their ability to integrate with existing systems without significant changes.
- B) Records of timely project completion and adherence to contractual obligations.
- C) Customer satisfaction ratings and feedback on the vendor's services.
- D) The scalability of the vendor's services to grow with your company.

Correct Answer: B

Explanation: Assessing a vendor's past performance, specifically their record of completing projects on time and adhering to the stipulations of contracts, is vital. It provides a reliable indicator of their operational reliability and commitment to fulfilling agreements, which can safeguard your project's success.

Question 244

Scenario: A company is considering a vendor for a large IT project. What is the most important initial step to take regarding due diligence?

- A) Reviewing the vendor's financial statements for the past five years.
- B) Conducting an initial risk assessment to identify potential security and compliance issues.
- C) Ensuring the vendor's proposal aligns with the project's scope and budget.
- D) Obtaining references from other clients who have used the vendor's services.

Correct Answer: B

Explanation: Conducting an initial risk assessment as a due diligence step helps in identifying potential security and compliance risks associated with the vendor. This proactive measure ensures that the vendor meets the necessary security standards to protect sensitive information and aligns with your company's risk management policies.

Question 245

Scenario: During a vendor review process, what aspect is crucial to verify to prevent future legal and security issues?

- A) Investigating any past data breaches or security incidents reported by the vendor.
- B) Ensuring the vendor has up-to-date and verified security certifications.
- C) Checking that the vendor does not employ individuals previously convicted of cyber crimes.
- D) Verifying the vendor's policies on data handling and employee training.

Correct Answer: B

Explanation: Ensuring that a vendor has up-to-date and verified security certifications is critical during the vendor review process. It helps in preventing future legal and security issues by confirming that the vendor follows best practices and meets industry-standard security requirements, which is fundamental in protecting your data and systems from threats.

Question 246

What is the most effective way to present a business case for security investment to stakeholders?

- A) Highlighting the financial benefits and risk mitigation provided by the proposed security investments.
- B) Outlining the new features and updates in existing security tools.

- C) Discussing the compliance requirements and penalties for non-adherence.
- D) Detailing the technical specifications and capabilities of new security technologies.

Correct Answer: A

Explanation: Highlighting the financial benefits and risk mitigation effectively demonstrates to stakeholders the tangible returns and protection offered by the security investment, making it a compelling argument for approval.

Question 247

Fill in the blank: In building a business case, it is crucial to quantify the _____ to convey the potential financial impact of security threats.

- A) The operational downtime caused by security incidents.
- B) The impact on customer trust and market reputation.
- C) Financial risks associated with potential security breaches.
- D) The speed of recovery from potential cyber-attacks.

Correct Answer: C

Explanation: Quantifying financial risks associated with potential security breaches helps stakeholders understand the direct impact of security threats in monetary terms, which is crucial for making informed investment decisions.

Question 248

How should a security professional demonstrate the return on investment (ROI) for security tools and measures to stakeholders?

- A) Comparing the cost of potential data breaches against the investment in security infrastructure.

- B) Evaluating the technological advancements in security tools over the past year.
- C) Highlighting the compliance benefits and avoidance of regulatory fines.
- D) Showcasing user testimonials and case studies of successful security implementations.

Correct Answer: A

Explanation: Demonstrating ROI by comparing potential loss from data breaches with the investment in security provides a clear, quantifiable metric that can persuade stakeholders of the financial prudence of the proposed measures.

Question 249

Scenario: You are tasked with justifying the need for an advanced threat detection system in your annual budget. What should be the focus of your presentation to stakeholders?

- A) Focusing on the technological superiority of the system compared to current solutions.
- B) Emphasizing the reduction in risk and potential financial losses from future threats.
- C) Illustrating the technical specifications and compliance benefits of the system.
- D) Detailing the cost implications of the system without discussing its benefits.

Correct Answer: B

Explanation: When proposing an advanced threat detection system, emphasizing the potential reduction in financial losses from future threats aligns with stakeholders' priority to protect financial assets, making the investment appealing.

Question 250

Scenario: If a company suffered a significant data breach last year, what key point should be highlighted when proposing enhanced security measures?

- A) Citing recent industry trends in cybersecurity threats and responses.

- B) Outlining the operational efficiencies gained through improved security practices.
- C) Explaining the enhancements in customer data protection and compliance adherence.
- D) Demonstrating how previous security breaches have led to financial losses and reputational damage.

Correct Answer: D

Explanation: Highlighting the financial and reputational damage from past breaches provides a strong, relatable rationale for enhanced security measures, stressing the need to prevent similar incidents to maintain company stability and market position.

Question 251

What is the primary benefit of using AI in cybersecurity?

- A) Improving compliance with regulatory requirements by documenting all security incidents.
- B) Enhancing the ability to identify and respond to threats more quickly than traditional methods.
- C) Increasing the efficiency of incident resolution by automating the analysis process.
- D) Reducing the workload on cybersecurity staff by automating routine tasks.

Correct Answer: B

Explanation: AI significantly enhances the speed and accuracy with which cybersecurity systems can identify and respond to threats, making it an invaluable tool for preemptively addressing potential risks before they can cause harm.

Question 252

Fill in the blank: AI enhances cybersecurity defenses by enabling the system to _____ threats in real-time.

- A) Generate detailed reports on potential security breaches
- B) Predict future vulnerabilities and patch them
- C) Automatically detect and respond to
- D) Monitor network traffic for unusual patterns

Correct Answer: C

Explanation: AI's real-time processing capabilities allow for the immediate detection and response to threats, greatly reducing the window of opportunity for cyber attackers to exploit vulnerabilities in the network.

Question 253
How does AI contribute to improving the accuracy of threat detection?

- A) By streamlining the communication between different security platforms.
- B) By decreasing false positives and negatives, thus saving time for security analysts.
- C) By learning from previous data to recognize patterns that may indicate potential threats.
- D) By applying complex algorithms to evaluate the severity of detected anomalies.

Correct Answer: C

Explanation: AI improves threat detection accuracy by utilizing machine learning to analyze vast quantities of data, learning from past incidents to identify patterns and anomalies that may signify potential threats, thus enhancing the predictive capabilities of cybersecurity systems.

Question 254

Scenario: When integrating AI into a cybersecurity system, what is a critical factor for ensuring its effectiveness in threat prediction?

- A) Regularly updating the AI algorithms to adapt to new threats and changing tactics.
- B) Incorporating feedback mechanisms to continuously improve AI predictions.
- C) Training the cybersecurity team to manually review AI-generated security alerts.
- D) Ensuring the AI system has access to comprehensive and up-to-date threat intelligence.

Correct Answer: D

Explanation: For AI to effectively predict and mitigate threats, it must be continually fed with the latest and most comprehensive threat intelligence available. This ensures the AI tools are up-to-date with the newest threat vectors and have the necessary data to make accurate predictions.

Question 255

Scenario: Your company is deploying AI for cybersecurity. What key step should be taken first to ensure its successful implementation?

- A) Integrating the AI system with existing security infrastructure without customization.
- B) Conducting a thorough security assessment to determine the current security posture and identify specific needs.
- C) Establishing a dedicated AI response team to manage alerts and updates.
- D) Implementing AI in non-critical areas first to evaluate its performance before full deployment.

Correct Answer: B

Explanation: Conducting a thorough security assessment prior to deploying AI tools ensures that the specific security needs are addressed and that the AI implementations are tailored to meet those needs effectively, thereby optimizing the security infrastructure.

Question 256

How does Machine Learning enhance the capability of security systems to detect new threats?

- A) Increasing the speed of incident response by automating the decision-making process.
- B) Streamlining compliance by ensuring all security measures adhere to regulatory requirements.
- C) Facilitating proactive security measures by predicting potential attack vectors in advance.
- D) By analyzing patterns and anomalies in data to identify unusual behaviors that may indicate threats.

Correct Answer: D

Explanation: Machine learning enhances threat detection by analyzing data patterns and anomalies, allowing security systems to identify and react to unusual behaviors indicative of new threats. This capability is crucial for detecting sophisticated cyber attacks that may not be identified by traditional signature-based methods.

Question 257

Fill in the blank: ML improves cybersecurity efficiency by automating the process of _____ across networks.

- A) security policy enforcement
- B) data encryption and secure communication
- C) log management and compliance tracking
- D) threat detection and analysis

Correct Answer: D

Explanation: Automating threat detection and analysis allows ML to rapidly analyze large volumes of network data in real time, identifying threats more quickly and efficiently than human analysts, thereby improving the overall efficiency of cybersecurity operations.

Question 258

What is a key advantage of implementing machine learning in cybersecurity regarding false positives?

- A) Increasing the alert generation speed to ensure faster response times to potential threats.
- B) Reducing the number of false positives by learning from previous security incidents to better distinguish between benign and malicious activities.
- C) Enhancing the ability of security personnel to manually review and address alerts.
- D) Improving the user interface of security systems to make them more accessible to non-technical staff.

Correct Answer: B

Explanation: Machine learning algorithms can learn from previous false positives and adjust their threat detection criteria, which significantly reduces the number of incorrect alerts. This improvement helps security teams focus on genuine threats and enhances overall security response effectiveness.

Question 259

Scenario: A company wants to implement ML to monitor and analyze user behavior for insider threats. What is an essential consideration for this application?

- A) Integrating the ML system with existing network security tools to enhance data collection.
- B) Ensuring that the ML system is trained on comprehensive and diverse data sets to accurately model normal user behavior.
- C) Configuring privacy controls to protect sensitive user data analyzed by the ML system.
- D) Regularly updating the algorithm parameters to adapt to evolving security threats.

Correct Answer: B

Explanation: When implementing ML for insider threat detection, it is crucial to train the system on comprehensive and diverse data sets. This training enables the system to accurately understand and predict normal versus anomalous user behaviors, reducing the risk of false positives and negatives.

Question 260

Scenario: If a security team is evaluating different ML models to predict phishing attacks, what should be the primary focus of their analysis?

- A) Evaluating the accuracy and precision of the models to ensure they effectively identify phishing attempts without generating excessive false alarms.
- B) Determining the cost-effectiveness of deploying each model in terms of resources and time.
- C) Analyzing the training time required for the models to become fully operational and effective.
- D) Assessing the scalability of the models to handle large volumes of data without performance degradation.

Correct Answer: A

Explanation: When evaluating ML models for phishing detection, focusing on the accuracy and precision of the models is essential. This ensures that the models can effectively identify real phishing attempts while minimizing the rate of false alarms, which is critical for maintaining operational efficiency and trust in the ML system.

Question 261

What is the fundamental principle of Zero Trust architecture?

- A) Never trust, always verify every access request, regardless of location.

- B) Encrypt data at rest and in transit across the network.
- C) Regularly update and patch all systems and software.
- D) Implement strong authentication methods for all users and devices.

Correct Answer: A

Explanation: The core principle of Zero Trust architecture is "never trust, always verify," which mandates that all access requests must be authenticated, authorized, and continuously validated for security configuration and posture before access is granted, regardless of the user's location.

Question 262

Fill in the blank: In a zero-trust model, it is crucial to continuously _____ both user and device security postures.

- A) evaluate and adjust
- B) verify and authenticate
- C) monitor and log
- D) assess and respond

Correct Answer: B

Explanation: Continuous verification and authentication of both user and device security postures are critical in a zero-trust model to ensure that the security status is up-to-date and to prevent unauthorized access that could lead to a security breach.

Question 263

What should be the primary focus when deploying microsegmentation under zero trust architecture?

- A) Creating a unified security policy that applies across all network segments.
- B) Integrating advanced threat intelligence tools for real-time threat analysis.
- C) Ensuring granular access control to limit lateral movement within the network.
- D) Applying machine learning algorithms to predict and prevent breaches.

Correct Answer: C

Explanation: Implementing granular access control in microsegmentation is essential in a zero-trust model to prevent unauthorized lateral movement within the network. This approach helps in minimizing the potential damage from breaches by tightly controlling access to different parts of the network.

Question 264

Scenario: Your organization is planning to implement Zero Trust for its cloud environments. What is the first step in deploying this model effectively?

- A) Conducting a pilot project to test Zero Trust principles on a small scale.
- B) Identifying all users and their access rights within the organization.
- C) Establishing a continuous monitoring system to track all network traffic.
- D) Developing a comprehensive inventory of all assets and their connectivity.

Correct Answer: D

Explanation: When deploying Zero Trust in cloud environments, developing a comprehensive inventory of all assets and their connectivity is crucial as it provides a clear view of what needs protection and how data flows across the network, which is fundamental for defining and enforcing security policies.

Question 265

Scenario: A company is considering transitioning to a Zero Trust architecture. What critical aspect must they evaluate to ensure effective implementation?

- A) Reviewing compliance requirements to ensure the new architecture meets all legal standards.
- B) Assessing the current security infrastructure to identify existing vulnerabilities.
- C) Upgrading encryption protocols and ensuring all data is protected in transit.
- D) Implementing robust network segmentation to reduce the attack surface.

Correct Answer: B

Explanation: Evaluating the current security infrastructure is vital for organizations considering transitioning to Zero Trust to identify any existing vulnerabilities that need to be addressed. This assessment helps in understanding the gaps in the current security setup that the Zero Trust model can fill, ensuring a smoother and more effective implementation.

Question 266

Which blockchain feature is essential for ensuring the integrity of security logs in distributed networks?

- A) Peer-to-peer network architecture allows for data to be distributed but not centralized, enhancing fault tolerance.
- B) Time-stamping of blocks which records the exact time a block was added to the blockchain, aiding in the chronological tracking of data.
- C) Cryptographic hash functions ensure that any alteration to the data within a block would result in a noticeable change to the block's hash.
- D) Consensus protocols which ensure all transactions are agreed upon by the nodes in the network before they are recorded.

Correct Answer: C

Explanation: Cryptographic hash functions are crucial for maintaining the integrity of security logs in blockchain. Any attempt to alter logged data alters the hash of the block, which is easily detectable and prevents tampering.

Question 267

Fill in the blank: In blockchain technology, the security of a transaction record is enhanced by chaining blocks using _____.

- A) Encryption standards that govern how data is encrypted within the blockchain, securing the data at rest.
- B) Block creation time that dictates how quickly new data or transactions are added to the blockchain.
- C) Cryptographic hashes that link each block to its predecessor, creating a secure and unbreakable chain.
- D) Smart contracts automatically execute, control, or document legally relevant events according to the terms of a contract or an agreement.

Correct Answer: C

Explanation: Cryptographic hashes create a chain-like structure by linking each new block with the previous one through their hashes. This ensures that any tampering with the data would invalidate the hashes, preserving the integrity of the entire blockchain.

Question 268

A company is assessing how blockchain can enhance their network security. They focus on how blockchain can prevent unauthorized data alterations. What is a fundamental blockchain mechanism that directly contributes to this?

- A) Decentralized nature of blockchain, which prevents any single point of control or failure, enhancing the robustness of the network.
- B) Hash rate which refers to the speed at which a block is discovered and the rate at which the related mathematics problem is solved.
- C) The immutable ledger that blockchain technology provides ensures that once a block is added to the chain, the data it contains cannot be altered retroactively without a consensus from the network.

- D) Public key infrastructure that supports the distribution and identification of public encryption keys, enabling secure data exchange.

Correct Answer: C

Explanation: The immutability of blockchain's ledger makes it ideal for securing data against unauthorized alterations. Once data has been added to the blockchain, changing it without consensus is computationally impractical, thus securing data from tampering.

Question 269

Consider a scenario where a security team needs to ensure the authenticity and non-repudiation of transactions across a decentralized network. What blockchain attribute is crucial for this purpose?

- A) Role-based access controls that define who can view or alter information on the blockchain network.
- B) Public-private key cryptography ensures that each participant can securely interact with the network without exposing sensitive information.
- C) Blockchain explorer tools allow users to view all past transactions, enhancing transparency but not specifically ensuring authenticity.
- D) Digital signatures used in blockchain help to verify the transaction's originator, ensuring that the transaction is both authenticated and unchangeable once recorded.

Correct Answer: D

Explanation: Digital signatures provide a mechanism to ensure that the transactions are authentic and that they cannot be repudiated once committed to the blockchain, addressing both authentication and non-repudiation.

Question 270

In a blockchain-based system, a security analyst needs to verify the validity of the entire blockchain to prevent tampering. What feature of blockchain is primarily used for this purpose?

- A) Distributed ledger technology that provides multiple copies of the blockchain across different nodes, making it difficult to tamper with.
- B) Multi-signature protocols require more than one key to authorize a transaction, adding an extra layer of security to blockchain transactions.
- C) Consensus algorithms which require multiple parties to agree on the state of the blockchain ledger, ensuring that any additions or changes are valid and recognized by all parties.
- D) The ability to create private blockchains, which restrict the participation in the network to only invited members.

Correct Answer: C

Explanation: Consensus algorithms are fundamental in blockchain operations as they require agreement among all nodes in the network before any change is accepted on the blockchain. This makes unauthorized changes virtually impossible without a majority control over the network, thereby securing the blockchain from tampering.

Question 271

What type of automation tool is most effective in minimizing response time during an incident in a security operations center?

- A) Managed detection and response (MDR) systems that offer outsourced monitoring and automated response features.
- B) Endpoint detection and response (EDR) systems that monitor and respond to suspicious activities on endpoint devices.
- C) Security orchestration and automation response (SOAR) platforms that integrate and automate various tools and processes in security operations.
- D) Network intrusion detection systems (NIDS) that automate the process of flagging suspicious network traffic.

Correct Answer: C

Explanation: Security orchestration and automation response (SOAR) platforms are specifically designed to integrate multiple security tools and automate incident response workflows. This reduces the manual effort required during an incident, which helps minimize response times and streamline processes across different security systems.

Question 272

Fill in the blank: Autonomous security operations utilize _____ to analyze and respond to threats without requiring human intervention.

- A) Data analytics engines that evaluate threat data and make recommendations to improve overall security posture.
- B) Rule-based engines that execute pre-programmed scripts to handle common threats and notify human operators of the outcomes.
- C) Behavior analytics tools that use statistical methods to detect abnormal activities but lack real-time response capabilities.
- D) Machine learning algorithms that continuously learn from previous incidents to enhance real-time decision-making and threat response.

Correct Answer: D

Explanation: Machine learning algorithms enable autonomous security operations by continuously learning from past incidents and adjusting their responses to new threats. These algorithms can make faster, more accurate decisions than manual processes, allowing for a more efficient defense against evolving threats.

Question 273

A company wants to integrate an automated solution to handle repetitive tasks in its incident response process. What kind of security tool is designed to streamline this function?

- A) Threat intelligence platforms that automate the collection, correlation, and dissemination of threat information.
- B) Cloud-based monitoring systems that provide real-time threat detection and allow remote automation of security protocols.
- C) Security orchestration platforms that automatically execute predefined actions based on detection triggers to reduce response times and errors.
- D) User and entity behavior analytics (UEBA) systems that flag outliers in behavior but rely on manual review for confirmation.

Correct Answer: C

Explanation: Security orchestration platforms are built to automate incident response processes. They automatically trigger predefined actions based on detection events, reducing the workload on security teams and improving response times to incidents like phishing attacks or malware detection.

Question 274

In a scenario where a company experiences a large-scale phishing attack, their security operations team needs to quickly isolate affected systems and respond to the threat. What feature of an automated incident response tool would be most beneficial in this situation?

- A) Automated threat intelligence feeds that gather and disseminate information to the response team without manual input.
- B) Incident isolation protocols built into the SOAR tool that can automatically contain and isolate compromised systems upon detecting abnormal behavior.
- C) Backup recovery systems that automatically restore affected data but require manual decisions to trigger these actions.
- D) Incident response dashboards that provide a high-level overview of threats but require manual intervention to take action.

Correct Answer: B

Explanation: In this case, an automated incident isolation protocol would allow the system to quickly isolate compromised systems without waiting for human intervention. This feature is critical in large-scale attacks, where speed is essential to contain the damage and limit the spread of the threat.

Question 275

A security analyst is setting up an automated response system for malware detection in a complex environment. What capability of an autonomous security operations tool would allow it to proactively contain threats and respond faster than a manual process?

- A) Static detection systems that flag known signatures and follow up with alert-based notifications to relevant personnel.
- B) Adaptive response mechanisms that detect, isolate, and neutralize malware in real-time across multiple environments, adjusting responses based on evolving threat landscapes.
- C) Manual override systems that allow the human analyst to intervene and take control of security operations at any point in the process.
- D) Centralized log management tools that store and analyze logs from multiple systems to identify and correlate anomalies.

Correct Answer: B

Explanation: Adaptive response mechanisms are vital in modern security environments because they allow automated systems to respond to malware threats in real time. By detecting and isolating malware across multiple systems, these tools help prevent the spread of threats and reduce the reliance on manual responses, leading to faster and more effective incident resolution.

Question 276

Which security control is most critical when securing containerized applications in a cloud-native environment?

- A) Vulnerability management platforms that continuously scan cloud-native environments for security risks and help prioritize remediation efforts.
- B) Identity and access management controls that strictly regulate who can access and modify cloud-native resources, ensuring that only authorized users interact with the

environment.
- C) Network segmentation ensures that traffic between containers is properly controlled and limited, reducing the attack surface in a cloud-native environment.
- D) Encryption at rest to ensure that any data stored within containers remains protected from unauthorized access.

Correct Answer: C

Explanation: Network segmentation is a key security control in cloud-native environments, particularly for containerized applications. It limits the communication between different containers and services, reducing the potential impact of an attack. By isolating workloads, network segmentation helps to minimize the attack surface and prevent unauthorized access between services.

Question 277

Fill in the blank: Cloud-native security often relies on _____ to provide runtime security by monitoring and protecting containerized workloads.

- A) Runtime protection that continuously monitors workloads, detecting and responding to abnormal behavior in real-time to prevent security breaches.
- B) Container firewalls that restrict network traffic in and out of individual containers, providing an extra layer of security.
- C) Intrusion detection systems (IDS) that monitor cloud-native infrastructure for signs of compromise and notify administrators when suspicious activity is detected.
- D) Dynamic access control systems that adapt permissions based on the current state of cloud-native workloads, ensuring flexible security policies.

Correct Answer: A

Explanation: Runtime protection tools are crucial in cloud-native security because they continuously monitor the behavior of workloads and containers while they are running. This allows for real-time detection of any anomalous or suspicious activity, enabling immediate response and protection against potential threats.

Question 278

A company is moving its services to a cloud-native architecture. They are concerned about securing the communication between microservices. What method can they implement to ensure secure communication in a cloud-native environment?

- A) Cloud security posture management (CSPM) tools that assess and improve the security posture of cloud-native assets, ensuring compliance with security standards.
- B) API gateways that enforce security policies and authenticate requests between microservices, ensuring secure communication in cloud-native environments.
- C) Token-based authentication which ensures secure and temporary access to cloud-native services, reducing the risk of compromised credentials.
- D) Mutual TLS (mTLS) encryption which ensures that both the client and server authenticate each other and that all communication between services remains encrypted.

Correct Answer: D

Explanation: Mutual TLS (mTLS) encryption ensures that both sides of a communication channel, such as microservices, are authenticated and that all communication is encrypted. This is essential in cloud-native environments where services constantly communicate with each other, as it prevents unauthorized access and protects the integrity of the data being exchanged.

Question 279

In a scenario where a DevOps team is deploying a new application in a cloud-native environment, they want to ensure the integrity of containers running in production. What cloud-native security practice should they apply to detect and prevent any unauthorized changes to containerized applications?

- A) Role-based access control (RBAC) to ensure that only authorized users can make changes to containerized applications.
- B) Immutable infrastructure to ensure that once a container is deployed, it cannot be modified, preventing unauthorized changes during runtime.

- C) Host-based intrusion prevention systems (HIPS) that monitor the underlying hosts of containerized applications, preventing unauthorized changes to the host environment.
- D) Image scanning tools that check containers for vulnerabilities before they are deployed, ensuring that only secure containers run in production.

Correct Answer: D

Explanation: Image scanning tools play a vital role in cloud-native security by scanning containers for vulnerabilities before they are deployed into production. This ensures that any known security flaws are identified and addressed, reducing the risk of deploying vulnerable containers that could be exploited during runtime.

Question 280

A security team is tasked with ensuring compliance in a cloud-native infrastructure where resources are dynamically created and destroyed. Which method should they adopt to maintain security policy enforcement across all cloud-native assets, regardless of their lifespan?

- A) Policy as code that automates the application of security policies across dynamic cloud-native resources, ensuring consistent policy enforcement regardless of how short-lived the resources are.
- B) Configuration management tools that ensure cloud-native resources are configured according to security best practices and compliance requirements.
- C) Log aggregation tools that collect security data from various cloud-native resources, making it easier to monitor and investigate potential security incidents.
- D) Dynamic secrets management which generates temporary credentials for accessing cloud-native resources, reducing the risk of long-term credential exposure.

Correct Answer: A

Explanation: Policy as code is an important method in cloud-native security because it allows security policies to be applied programmatically and consistently across all resources, even as they are dynamically created and destroyed. This ensures that security policies are enforced throughout the entire lifecycle of cloud-native resources, providing continuous protection.

Question 281

Which security measure is most effective for detecting lateral movement in an advanced persistent threat (APT) attack?

- A) External threat intelligence feeds to correlate data from known APT sources and identify potential attackers.
- B) East-west traffic monitoring to detect unauthorized movement between hosts within the network, making lateral movement easier to identify.
- C) Behavioral analytics systems that use machine learning to detect abnormal user and system behavior, which could indicate lateral movement.
- D) Honeypot systems to lure attackers and monitor their behavior without risking critical assets.

Correct Answer: B

Explanation: East-west traffic monitoring is a critical component for detecting lateral movement in APT attacks. Lateral movement refers to how attackers navigate through an internal network once they have gained initial access. By monitoring the traffic between internal systems, security teams can identify unusual behavior that may indicate an attacker moving within the network, even if traditional defenses have been bypassed.

Question 282

Fill in the blank: One of the most effective defenses against APT attacks is implementing _____ to segment networks and limit the movement of attackers within the environment.

- A) Vulnerability management tools that help organizations regularly patch and update vulnerable systems.
- B) Network segmentation which divides the network into smaller isolated segments to contain and limit an attacker's lateral movement after breaching the initial defense.
- C) Firewalls that enforce strict traffic rules, minimizing access to unauthorized systems.
- D) Zero-trust architecture that enforces continuous authentication and verification, even

within the network.

Correct Answer: B

Explanation: Network segmentation is an effective defense against APTs because it restricts the movement of attackers by isolating different parts of the network. When an APT gains access to one segment, they are unable to move freely to other segments without triggering security mechanisms. This containment strategy makes it harder for attackers to escalate privileges and reach sensitive data or systems.

Question 283

A company suspects that they are being targeted by an APT. The attackers are exfiltrating data slowly to avoid detection. What security control could help detect this stealthy data exfiltration?

- A) Data loss prevention (DLP) systems that monitor network traffic for unauthorized data exfiltration and flag suspicious activity that may indicate APTs.
- B) Endpoint detection and response (EDR) solutions that continuously monitor endpoints for signs of compromise.
- C) Network intrusion detection systems (NIDS) to detect abnormal traffic patterns that could indicate exfiltration.
- D) Host-based intrusion prevention systems (HIPS) that monitor for suspicious activities at the host level.

Correct Answer: A

Explanation: Data loss prevention (DLP) systems are designed to monitor for unauthorized data exfiltration, especially when attackers try to extract data in small amounts to evade detection. In the context of an APT, DLP can alert security teams to unusual data transfers that may indicate a slow, stealthy attack. This is particularly important when attackers use advanced techniques to avoid triggering traditional security alarms.

Question 284

In a scenario where an organization has identified an APT within their network, they must limit the attacker's ability to communicate with their command and control (C2) servers. What mitigation strategy should the security team apply to disrupt the C2 communication while investigating the APT?

- A) DNS sinkholing that redirects malicious DNS requests, preventing the attacker from communicating with their command and control servers.
- B) Network segmentation firewalls that isolate different sections of the network and prevent unauthorized access to critical areas.
- C) Intrusion detection systems (IDS) that monitor network traffic for known signatures associated with C2 communication.
- D) IP reputation services that block known malicious IP addresses from establishing connections.

Correct Answer: A

Explanation: DNS sinkholing is a powerful technique for disrupting command and control (C2) communications in APT attacks. By redirecting malicious DNS requests, a sinkhole prevents the attacker from communicating with their remote servers, effectively cutting off the attacker's ability to control compromised systems. This mitigation strategy buys time for the security team to investigate and respond to the APT without allowing the attackers to continue their operation.

Question 285

A security operations center (SOC) is investigating suspicious activity that suggests an ongoing APT attack. They want to capture and analyze the full lifecycle of the attack, including initial access, lateral movement, and persistence. What type of monitoring should the SOC implement to gain full visibility into the attacker's activities?

- A) Centralized logging and monitoring systems to collect and analyze log data from multiple systems and devices across the network.
- B) Full packet capture solutions that record all network traffic and enable deep analysis of APT activities across multiple stages of the attack.
- C) Security information and event management (SIEM) systems that aggregate and analyze

security logs in real-time to detect APT activities.
- D) Anomaly-based intrusion detection systems (IDS) that monitor for unusual patterns in network traffic, providing a high-level view of suspicious activities.

Correct Answer: B

Explanation: Full packet capture allows security teams to record and analyze all network traffic, providing visibility into every stage of an APT attack. This approach is critical for understanding the attacker's techniques, tactics, and procedures (TTPs) throughout the entire lifecycle of the attack. By capturing packets, analysts can trace the attack back to its initial entry point, track lateral movement, and identify persistence mechanisms, giving them the information they need to fully eradicate the threat.

Question 286

Which cryptographic algorithm is most vulnerable to attacks by quantum computers, requiring significant changes to ensure security in a post-quantum world?

- A) RSA encryption is vulnerable to quantum attacks, as quantum algorithms can factor large numbers exponentially faster, breaking the core mathematical basis of RSA.
- B) Elliptic Curve Cryptography (ECC), which relies on the difficulty of the elliptic curve discrete logarithm problem, making it vulnerable to quantum attacks.
- C) AES-256 encryption, which is still considered secure against quantum threats due to its symmetric key nature, though quantum computers can reduce the security margin.
- D) Blowfish, which is a symmetric key block cipher designed to be a fast, general-purpose encryption algorithm but lacks quantum resistance.

Correct Answer: A

Explanation: RSA encryption is vulnerable to quantum computing because Shor's algorithm can factor large numbers in polynomial time, which is exponentially faster than the best-known classical algorithms. RSA relies on the difficulty of factoring large integers, and quantum computing would render RSA encryption ineffective by breaking this fundamental assumption.

Question 287

Fill in the blank: Quantum computing could potentially break traditional encryption methods by using _____ to solve complex mathematical problems exponentially faster than classical computers.

- A) Quantum key distribution (QKD) that uses quantum mechanics to secure the exchange of cryptographic keys, making it immune to quantum computer attacks on encryption.
- B) Quantum annealing, which is used in quantum computers to solve optimization problems and accelerate specific calculations, but does not directly affect cryptography.
- C) Grover's algorithm, which speeds up brute-force attacks on symmetric key encryption by providing a quadratic speedup over classical search algorithms.
- D) Shor's algorithm, which is designed to solve integer factorization and discrete logarithm problems much faster on quantum computers than classical algorithms can.

Correct Answer: D

Explanation: Shor's algorithm is the key quantum algorithm that could disrupt current cryptographic systems. It is designed to solve both the integer factorization problem and the discrete logarithm problem efficiently, both of which are the basis for much of today's public-key cryptography, such as RSA and ECC. This makes traditional encryption highly vulnerable in a quantum computing context.

Question 288

A company is concerned about the future threat of quantum computers breaking their current encryption. They plan to transition to quantum-resistant algorithms. What type of cryptography should they adopt to protect their sensitive communications in a post-quantum era?

- A) Multivariate polynomial cryptography, which uses a system of multivariate polynomials that are difficult for both classical and quantum computers to solve.
- B) Lattice-based cryptography provides quantum resistance by relying on mathematical problems that are believed to be hard even for quantum computers to solve efficiently.

- C) Hash-based cryptography, which provides quantum resistance by securing data through hashing mechanisms that quantum algorithms struggle to reverse-engineer.
- D) Code-based cryptography, which is based on the hardness of decoding random linear codes, offering quantum resistance and being a candidate for post-quantum security.

Correct Answer: B

Explanation: Lattice-based cryptography is currently one of the most promising approaches for post-quantum cryptography. It is believed to resist quantum attacks because the mathematical problems it is based on, such as the Shortest Vector Problem (SVP), are difficult even for quantum computers to solve. This makes it a leading candidate for securing sensitive communications in a post-quantum world.

Question 289

In a scenario where an organization is preparing for the impact of quantum computing on its cryptographic infrastructure, they must ensure their current encrypted data remains secure against future quantum attacks. What proactive approach should the organization take to protect long-term sensitive data?

- A) Blockchain encryption systems that rely on distributed ledger technology to protect data integrity but are not inherently quantum-resistant.
- B) Post-quantum cryptographic migration strategies that focus on upgrading to quantum-resistant algorithms before quantum computers become a realistic threat.
- C) Key management systems that securely rotate encryption keys on a regular basis, ensuring that compromised keys do not expose large amounts of sensitive data.
- D) Quantum encryption techniques that protect data through quantum key distribution (QKD) but require specialized hardware and infrastructure to implement.

Correct Answer: B

Explanation: Post-quantum cryptographic migration involves adopting quantum-resistant encryption algorithms before quantum computers become widely available. This proactive approach ensures that long-term sensitive data, which may remain valuable for years to come, is protected from future quantum threats. Organizations can implement these algorithms early to ensure continued security.

Question 290

A security team is tasked with evaluating their organization's cryptographic protocols in light of the emerging threat of quantum computing. They want to implement a cryptosystem that combines traditional algorithms with quantum-resistant cryptography. What method should they use to ensure both near-term and long-term security?

- A) Symmetric key encryption systems that use larger key sizes to increase the difficulty of brute-forcing encryption even with quantum computational power.
- B) Multi-party encryption schemes that allow different entities to share encrypted data but do not provide quantum resistance on their own.
- C) Secure multiparty computation that allows parties to compute a function over their inputs while keeping those inputs private, offering some protection but not focused on quantum resilience.
- D) Hybrid cryptography that combines current public key algorithms with quantum-resistant encryption methods to ensure security against both classical and quantum threats.

Correct Answer: D

Explanation: Hybrid cryptography offers a practical solution for the transition to quantum-safe encryption. By combining traditional encryption methods with quantum-resistant algorithms, organizations can maintain security in the present while preparing for future quantum attacks. This method ensures that data is secure against both current classical threats and emerging quantum threats.

Question 291

What is a common use of deception technology in a networked environment to detect attackers attempting lateral movement?

- A) Intrusion detection systems (IDS) that detect and alert administrators of suspicious activities without misleading attackers.
- B) Decoy systems that mimic real services and systems, tricking attackers into revealing

their presence when they attempt lateral movement.
- C) Traffic analysis tools that monitor all network traffic for suspicious activity but do not use deception to mislead attackers.
- D) Endpoint detection systems that monitor activity on individual devices, preventing unauthorized access to the network but do not use decoys.

Correct Answer: B

Explanation: Decoy systems are a key element of deception technology. These systems mimic real services, such as file servers, databases, or web servers, but are set up solely to detect attackers. By interacting with these decoys, attackers reveal their presence and intentions, allowing security teams to take action before any real damage occurs.

Question 292

Fill in the blank: Deception technology can use _____ to create fake systems and services that lure attackers into interacting with non-critical assets.

- A) Honeypot systems that actively engage with attackers to collect information about their behavior and gather threat intelligence.
- B) Virtual firewalls that filter incoming and outgoing traffic, preventing unauthorized access to sensitive systems without deploying decoy assets.
- C) Cloud-based sandbox environments that test suspicious files and applications in an isolated environment without interacting with real systems.
- D) Fake assets that simulate real systems but are designed to detect and monitor attackers who interact with them.

Correct Answer: D

Explanation: Fake assets in deception technology are used to lure attackers into interacting with systems that are not critical to operations. These decoys are designed to look legitimate, encouraging attackers to engage with them, thus allowing security teams to observe and respond to malicious activities without risking the integrity of real assets.

Question 293

A company has deployed several decoy servers throughout their network to detect unauthorized activity. The security team observes abnormal behavior on one of these decoys. What action should the team take after identifying this behavior?

- A) Engage in active defense measures, such as disabling attacker communication channels and cutting off access to the network.
- B) Monitor the attacker's behavior closely to understand their methods while ensuring no real assets are affected by the attacker's activity.
- C) Automatically shut down the affected network segment to prevent any potential compromise of real systems.
- D) Erase any traces of the attacker's presence in the network by clearing logs and resetting systems to prevent further infiltration.

Correct Answer: B

Explanation: Monitoring the attacker's behavior in the decoy environment is essential for gathering intelligence. By allowing the attacker to interact with the decoy system, the security team can learn about the attack methods, tools, and techniques being used. This approach minimizes the risk to real assets, as the attacker is interacting only with a controlled, fake environment.

Question 294

In a scenario where a security team has implemented deception technology, they detect an attacker interacting with a decoy database that contains fictitious sensitive data. What is the best way for the team to gather intelligence on the attacker's techniques while limiting the risk to real systems?

- A) Deploy additional decoys throughout the network to further mislead and distract the attacker from critical systems.
- B) Immediately isolate the decoy system from the network to prevent any potential compromise of legitimate assets.
- C) Use the decoy to observe the attacker's behavior and gain valuable information about their techniques without alerting them to the deception.
- D) Initiate legal action against the attacker based on the gathered intelligence, working

with law enforcement to track the attacker's identity.

Correct Answer: C

Explanation: Observing the attacker's behavior in a decoy environment allows security teams to gather valuable intelligence without alerting the attacker. This method helps in understanding the attacker's strategies and provides critical information on how they operate, while keeping actual sensitive data and systems secure.

Question 295

A security operations center (SOC) is using deception technology to detect advanced persistent threats (APTs). After a successful alert from a decoy system, the SOC needs to analyze how the attacker compromised the decoy. What should the SOC monitor to gain insights into the attacker's methods and tactics?

- A) Review logs of all communication within the network and match them with known attack patterns to identify potential future threats.
- B) Track the attacker's use of tools and techniques as they interact with the decoy to learn how they exploit vulnerabilities and gain unauthorized access.
- C) Monitor external network connections to identify any outgoing communication from the decoy system to the attacker's command-and-control servers.
- D) Focus on the vulnerabilities exploited by the attacker and patch the real systems that may have similar weaknesses.

Correct Answer: B

Explanation: Tracking the attacker's use of tools and techniques within the decoy system helps the SOC analyze the methods used by the attacker. This allows the SOC to identify specific tactics, techniques, and procedures (TTPs) that the attacker is using, providing insights into how they might approach real systems, and helping the SOC strengthen defenses against future attacks.

Question 296

During a cybersecurity wargame exercise, which component is most important for testing the readiness of incident response teams to handle sophisticated attacks?

- A) Communication channels between departments to ensure that relevant personnel are informed about the attack and the necessary actions are coordinated effectively.
- B) Incident escalation procedures that ensure the response team is quickly notified of an ongoing attack and initiates containment measures.
- C) Network segmentation strategies that isolate critical systems, preventing attackers from easily moving laterally during a cyberattack.
- D) Endpoint detection and response tools that automatically detect and isolate infected systems without requiring human intervention.

Correct Answer: B

Explanation: Incident escalation procedures are crucial during wargames because they test how quickly the response team is notified of an attack and how effectively they can initiate containment. Early detection and fast response are key to minimizing the damage from sophisticated attacks, so this process ensures the team is fully prepared for real-world scenarios.

Question 297

Fill in the blank: Incident wargaming helps identify gaps in an organization's defenses by simulating _____ that mimic real-world attack scenarios.

- A) Breach detection alerts that notify the team when specific suspicious behaviors are detected in the system.
- B) Advanced attack techniques that test how well the organization can detect and respond to complex cyber-attacks in a realistic environment.
- C) Red team simulations that engage in active attacks, giving the blue team realistic practice in detecting and mitigating threats.
- D) Real-time incident logging that captures every action taken during the wargame, providing a detailed record for post-incident analysis.

Correct Answer: B

Explanation: Simulating advanced attack techniques during wargames provides valuable insights into how well an organization can handle real-world threats. These techniques often involve complex, evolving tactics, forcing teams to adapt quickly. This helps identify weaknesses in detection, response, and mitigation strategies.

Question 298

A company is conducting a wargame to simulate a ransomware attack. The simulation focuses on how quickly the incident response team can detect and contain the threat. What metric should be monitored to evaluate the effectiveness of the team's response?

- A) Time to detection, which measures how long it takes for the team to identify the ransomware threat within the network and initiate the response plan.
- B) User access control changes to prevent further spread of the ransomware to other parts of the network once detected.
- C) Backup and recovery strategies that help ensure that systems can be restored quickly after the encryption of critical files.
- D) Encryption recovery processes that determine how fast encrypted data can be restored from backups during a ransomware incident.

Correct Answer: A

Explanation: Time to detection is a critical metric in wargame simulations, especially during ransomware scenarios. It measures how long it takes for the team to detect the threat and begin mitigation efforts. A shorter detection time leads to faster containment, reducing the overall impact of the ransomware.

Question 299

In a scenario where a large organization is conducting a wargame simulating an advanced persistent threat (APT) attack, the attacker remains undetected in the network for an extended period. What part of the wargame should focus on improving detection and response capabilities in future scenarios?

- A) Incident response playbooks that provide predefined steps for handling various types of attacks, including APTs.
- B) Anomaly detection systems that analyze network traffic patterns and trigger alerts when deviations from normal activity are observed.
- C) Security information and event management (SIEM) systems that monitor and correlate logs to detect unusual activities over time.
- D) Threat-hunting exercises that improve the team's ability to actively search for hidden attackers within the network, enhancing detection of APT activities.

Correct Answer: D

Explanation: Threat-hunting exercises are an important part of wargames focused on APTs, as they involve actively searching for attackers who have evaded traditional defenses. Improving threat-hunting capabilities helps organizations detect hidden threats earlier and respond more effectively, which is crucial for handling advanced attacks like APTs.

Question 300

A security team is preparing for an incident wargame exercise. They want to simulate a supply chain attack, targeting third-party software the organization relies on. What aspect of the wargame should be emphasized to better assess the organization's preparedness for such an attack?

- A) Incident recovery plans that focus on restoring normal operations after a supply chain attack has compromised third-party software.
- B) Data integrity checks that verify the accuracy and security of critical data received from third-party vendors.
- C) Software patching protocols to ensure that vulnerabilities in third-party software are regularly addressed and do not provide an attack vector.
- D) Third-party risk management to assess how well the organization can handle a supply chain attack originating from external software or services.

Correct Answer: D

Explanation: Third-party risk management is essential during supply chain attack simulations. It assesses how well the organization can respond to threats originating from external vendors or software. This aspect ensures that the organization is prepared to handle attacks involving third-party dependencies, which are increasingly being targeted by attackers.

Question 301

Which of the following is a primary task when leading a cybersecurity program in a corporate environment?

- A) Implementing a robust digital forensic process to investigate breaches.
- B) Establishing and enforcing security policies tailored to the organization's needs.
- C) Conducting periodic training sessions for new and existing employees.
- D) Reviewing and updating the employee access control systems annually.

Correct Answer: B

Explanation: Establishing and enforcing tailored security policies is crucial as it ensures that specific organizational needs and risks are addressed directly, providing a structured and relevant approach to mitigating potential security issues.

Question 302

When maintaining a cybersecurity program, it is essential to assess risks. What method provides the most comprehensive insight into potential security threats?

- A) Bi-annual risk assessments conducted by the internal audit team.
- B) Automated continuous monitoring systems that provide real-time alerts and status reports.
- C) Annual reviews of policy compliance by an independent auditor.
- D) Quarterly manual penetration testing by an external provider.

Correct Answer: B

Explanation: Automated continuous monitoring provides real-time data and alerts about the organization's security posture, allowing for immediate reaction to threats and ongoing assessment of system integrity, which is vital for proactive threat management.

Question 303

Fill in the blank: The standard for incident response within a well-maintained cybersecurity program is to ____ within the first 24 hours after detection.

- A) compile a list of affected systems and potential vulnerabilities.
- B) organize a debrief with the crisis management team.
- C) draft and disseminate security alerts to all employees.
- D) establish a communication plan and initial assessment.

Correct Answer: D

Explanation: Establishing a communication plan and conducting an initial assessment are critical first steps after detecting an incident to manage the situation effectively and mitigate any potential damage or escalation.

Question 304

A cybersecurity manager is revising the disaster recovery plan. Which of these should be prioritized to align with business continuity requirements?

- A) Overhauling the entire network architecture to improve security.
- B) Integrating advanced threat intelligence tools into the existing infrastructure.
- C) Ensuring that backup systems are regularly tested and meet the recovery time objectives.
- D) Updating antivirus software and deploying new firewalls across the network.

Correct Answer: C

Explanation: Regular testing of backup systems ensures that they are functional and effective in a disaster scenario, aligning with business continuity plans to minimize downtime and operational disruption.

Question 305

During a routine audit of the cybersecurity program, which metric would be most indicative of the program's effectiveness in terms of incident management?

- A) The ratio of incidents resolved within the predetermined service level agreement timeframe.
- B) Percentage of employees who have completed annual security training.
- C) Number of security patches applied within a month of release.
- D) Total cost associated with security breaches over the past fiscal year.

Correct Answer: A

Explanation: Tracking the ratio of incidents resolved within the agreed service level agreement timeframe offers a clear measure of the incident management's responsiveness and effectiveness, reflecting directly on the cybersecurity program's success in maintaining operational standards.

Question 306

What is the primary purpose of aligning IT strategies with business objectives in cybersecurity governance?

- A) To guarantee that technology investments directly increase shareholder value.
- B) To ensure that the organization's security measures enhance business efficiency and

risk management.
- C) To minimize IT operational costs irrespective of business outcomes.
- D) To isolate IT planning and operations from business strategy to streamline technical performance.

Correct Answer: B

Explanation: Aligning IT strategies with business objectives is fundamental to enhancing business efficiency and managing risk effectively. This alignment ensures that cybersecurity measures support overall business goals, not just technical requirements, thus fostering a secure yet flexible operational environment that drives business growth.

Question 307

When setting up an IT governance framework, what is the most critical factor for ensuring IT strategies support business goals?

- A) Establishing IT policies that operate independently of business strategies.
- B) Prioritizing technology trends over business strategy alignment.
- C) Effective communication between IT and business stakeholders.
- D) The speed of technology deployment without regard to its alignment with business objectives.

Correct Answer: C

Explanation: Effective communication between IT and business stakeholders is crucial because it ensures that IT strategies are developed with a clear understanding of business goals and needs. This alignment is essential for the successful implementation of IT initiatives that support and drive business objectives.

Question 308

Fill in the blank: In IT governance, the role of Chief Information Security Officer (CISO) primarily involves ensuring that all IT security policies and procedures ____ with the overall business strategy.

- A) adhere strictly to regulatory compliance.
- B) align closely and effectively.
- C) be implemented without customization or consultation.
- D) focus solely on technological innovation.

Correct Answer: B

Explanation: Ensuring that IT security policies and procedures align with business strategy is key to the role of a CISO. This alignment helps in maintaining security measures that support and do not hinder business objectives, ensuring that security strategies are not only preventative but also additive to business efficiency and growth.

Question 309

During a strategic review, the IT department proposes a new security technology that is expensive but offers advanced features. How should the decision be made to align with business objectives?

- A) Evaluate the technology's potential ROI relative to its cost and strategic benefits to the business.
- B) Follow industry trends rather than specific business needs.
- C) Base the decision on the preferences of the IT department's senior management.
- D) Choose the cheapest available solution to minimize expenditure.

Correct Answer: A

Explanation: Evaluating the potential ROI of new technology against its costs and strategic benefits is crucial in decision-making processes that align IT with business objectives. This approach ensures that investments in technology are justified by their expected benefits to the organization's strategic goals, optimizing resource allocation and enhancing business value.

Question 310

The company plans to expand into new markets, requiring changes to its IT infrastructure. What is the first step in ensuring the IT strategy supports this business objective?

- A) Conduct a needs analysis to determine the specific IT requirements of the new markets.
- B) Seek input from IT vendors on what technology to deploy.
- C) Implement the most advanced technology available to outpace competitors.
- D) Delay any IT upgrades until the market expansion has proven successful.

Correct Answer: A

Explanation: Conducting a needs analysis as the first step when planning IT infrastructure changes for market expansion ensures that the IT strategy is tailored to support new business objectives efficiently and effectively. This initial step helps identify specific requirements and potential challenges, paving the way for more informed and strategic IT planning that aligns with business expansion goals.

Question 311

What is the first step in designing an effective information security program for a large corporation?

- A) Defining the roles and responsibilities within the security team.
- B) Recruiting a team of experienced cybersecurity professionals.
- C) Conducting a thorough risk assessment to identify potential threats and vulnerabilities.
- D) Establishing a budget for cybersecurity tools and software.

Correct Answer: C

Explanation: Conducting a thorough risk assessment as the first step is critical because it allows the organization to identify and evaluate potential threats and vulnerabilities specific to its operations. This assessment forms the foundation upon which a tailored and effective security program can be built, ensuring that resources are allocated effectively to mitigate significant risks.

Question 312

When building a new security program, which factor is most critical for ensuring the security measures are robust and comprehensive?

- A) Focusing primarily on endpoint security to prevent data breaches.
- B) Limiting access to sensitive information to a small group of employees.
- C) Prioritizing user training over technological solutions.
- D) Integration of security controls at every layer of the IT infrastructure.

Correct Answer: D

Explanation: Integrating security controls at every layer of the IT infrastructure ensures that there are no weak points that could be exploited by attackers. This comprehensive approach to security architecture helps to protect the organization's data and systems from a wide range of potential attacks by creating multiple layers of defense.

Question 313

Fill in the blank: To ensure scalability and adaptability, security programs should be designed with _____ as a core principle.

- A) flexibility and modularity.
- B) reliance on automated tools.
- C) continuous improvement feedback loops.
- D) strict adherence to regulatory compliance.

Correct Answer: A

Explanation: Designing security programs with flexibility and modularity allows an organization to adapt to changes in the threat landscape or business needs without undergoing complete overhauls. This approach provides the ability to scale security measures up or down and to incorporate new technologies or processes as they become necessary, thereby maintaining long-term security effectiveness.

Question 314

A company is transitioning from a traditional on-premises IT infrastructure to a hybrid cloud model. What must be prioritized in the security program to protect both environments effectively?

- A) Segregating data storage between cloud and on-premises solutions.
- B) Increasing the encryption level for data transferred to the cloud.
- C) Development of a unified security policy that addresses the specific needs of both environments.
- D) Enhancing the physical security measures at data centers.

Correct Answer: C

Explanation: Developing a unified security policy for hybrid environments is crucial because it ensures consistent security postures across both on-premises and cloud components. This policy should address the specific needs and risks of both environments, providing a cohesive framework that helps prevent security gaps and ensures comprehensive protection.

Question 315

During a program development meeting, a security analyst suggests integrating an AI-driven threat detection system. What should be evaluated first before implementation?

- A) The cost-effectiveness of the AI system compared to traditional methods.

- B) The AI system's ability to reduce false positives in threat detection.
- C) The compatibility of the AI system with existing security infrastructure.
- D) The speed of implementation of the AI system into the current processes.

Correct Answer: C

Explanation: Evaluating the compatibility of an AI-driven threat detection system with the existing security infrastructure is essential before implementation. This ensures that the new system can integrate smoothly with current tools and processes, leveraging existing assets, and enhancing the organization's security posture without causing disruptions or introducing new vulnerabilities.

Question 316

What is a critical factor to consider when designing a secure network topology for a financial institution?

- A) Placement of all servers in a single, highly secure physical location.
- B) Utilization of a single firewall at the network perimeter for simplicity.
- C) Implementing a flat network design to facilitate easier management.
- D) Incorporation of redundant pathways to ensure availability even in the event of an attack.

Correct Answer: D

Explanation: Incorporating redundant pathways in a network topology, especially for a financial institution, ensures that the network remains operational and secure even if one part is compromised or goes down. This is crucial for maintaining availability and security, essential for financial transactions which require high reliability and protection against interruptions and attacks.

Question 317

In crafting a robust information security architecture, which element is essential for ensuring data integrity during transmission?

- A) Periodic checksums to verify data integrity post-transmission.
- B) Use of end-to-end encryption for all data in transit.
- C) Application of digital signatures to verify the authenticity of data.
- D) Relying solely on antivirus software to protect data integrity.

Correct Answer: B

Explanation: Using end-to-end encryption for data in transit protects data integrity by ensuring that data sent across a network is encrypted from the sender to the recipient, preventing unauthorized access and ensuring that the data cannot be altered without detection during transmission. This is fundamental in any robust security architecture to safeguard sensitive information.

Question 318

Fill in the blank: Effective segmentation of a network is essential in security architecture because it helps to _____ in the event of a breach.

- A) optimize the speed of data transmission across the network.
- B) contain potential threats and limit access to critical assets.
- C) reduce the overall cost of security management and monitoring.
- D) increase the complexity of the network structure unnecessarily.

Correct Answer: B

Explanation: Effective network segmentation helps contain potential threats by limiting their access to adjacent network segments, thus protecting critical assets from widespread compromise. This isolation reduces the attack surface and helps manage and mitigate risks more effectively, which is particularly crucial in extensive enterprise environments.

Question 319

A company is deploying a new service that handles sensitive customer data. What security architecture decision must be prioritized to ensure data protection?

- A) Integrating a single sign-on system to simplify user access management.
- B) Implementation of strong access controls and encryption for data at rest and in transit.
- C) Deployment of network intrusion detection systems at key data endpoints.
- D) Adopting a less restrictive firewall policy to ensure uninterrupted service.

Correct Answer: B

Explanation: Prioritizing strong access controls and encryption for both data at rest and in transit is essential when deploying new services that handle sensitive information. These measures ensure that data is accessible only to authorized individuals and remains confidential and intact, providing a high level of security against unauthorized access and data breaches.

Question 320

An organization is reviewing its security architecture due to increased regulatory requirements. What should be the first step in this process?

- A) Conducting an internal audit to identify potential insider threats.
- B) Assessment of current security measures against the new regulatory standards.
- C) Review of user access levels and permissions across the organization.
- D) Immediate update of all software to the latest versions available.

Correct Answer: B

Explanation: Assessing current security measures against new regulatory requirements is a critical first step in ensuring compliance. This assessment helps identify gaps in the existing architecture and guides the necessary enhancements or modifications to meet increased regulatory demands, thereby maintaining the organization's legal and operational standing.

Question 321

What is the primary benefit of implementing the least privilege principle in an access control system?

- A) It enhances system performance by reducing the number of users accessing large files.
- B) It allows for easier auditing and tracking of user activities across the system.
- C) It simplifies the management of user permissions by applying broad access rights.
- D) It minimizes the risk of data breaches by restricting user access to the resources necessary for their roles.

Correct Answer: D

Explanation: Implementing the least privilege principle is fundamental in minimizing the risk of unauthorized access and potential data breaches. By ensuring that users only have access to resources essential for their specific roles, the organization significantly reduces the attack surface and the possibility of internal and external threats exploiting excessive permissions.

Question 322

In the context of RBAC, what is the most important factor to consider when defining roles?

- A) The job functions and responsibilities within the organization.
- B) The technical skills and certifications that employees hold.
- C) The geographical location of employees and the time zones they work in.
- D) The seniority level of employees in the company.

Correct Answer: A

Explanation: When defining roles in an RBAC system, it is crucial to base them on the actual job functions and responsibilities within the organization. This approach ensures that access rights are aligned with business needs and job requirements, which enhances security and operational efficiency without granting excessive or insufficient permissions.

Question 323

Fill in the blank: In RBAC, roles should be designed based on _____ rather than individual user preferences.

- A) seniority or titles within the company.
- B) the length of time an employee has been with the company.
- C) personal interests or previous job experiences.
- D) job functions and responsibilities.   .

Correct Answer: D

Explanation: Designing roles based on job functions and responsibilities ensures that each role has access rights that are necessary and sufficient to perform their duties. This alignment avoids the pitfalls of basing access on less relevant factors like seniority, which might not accurately reflect the user's needs or organizational security requirements.

Question 324

A new software development project requires access to a version control system. How should access be assigned based on RBAC principles?

- A) Assign access to all team members to ensure full transparency and collaboration.
- B) Allow open access initially and restrict it only if issues arise.
- C) Grant access on a temporary basis and review permissions periodically.
- D) Create roles corresponding to different job functions within the team and assign access accordingly.

Correct Answer: D

Explanation: In RBAC, when a new project starts, it is important to define roles according to the job functions of the team members involved. This method ensures that access to systems, like a version control system, is granted appropriately based on the user's role and responsibilities in the project, thus adhering to both the principles of least privilege and effective project management.

Question 325

During an audit, it was found that an employee could access financial records not required for their role. What is the first corrective action using RBAC?

- A) Review and adjust the roles to ensure they align with the principle of least privilege.
- B) Implement stricter password policies to prevent unauthorized access.
- C) Increase the monitoring of user activities to detect any inappropriate access.
- D) Conduct a training session for all employees about security policies.

Correct Answer: A

Explanation: The first corrective action after finding excessive permissions during an audit is to review and adjust the roles to realign with the least privilege principle. This step involves ensuring that each role only grants access to the resources that are necessary for the role's responsibilities, effectively mitigating the risk of unauthorized access or data leaks by aligning roles more closely with actual job requirements.

Question 326

What is the primary objective of implementing a structured change management process in IT security?

- A) To expedite the implementation of new technologies without thorough testing.
- B) To create more work for the IT security team by introducing frequent changes.
- C) To minimize potential disruptions by ensuring all changes are systematically analyzed and implemented.

- D) To increase the frequency of changes in the security settings to test system resilience.

Correct Answer: C

Explanation: Implementing a structured change management process is crucial for minimizing potential disruptions by ensuring that all changes are systematically analyzed, planned, and implemented. This process helps in maintaining stability in IT operations and enhances security by preventing unintended consequences of poorly managed changes.

Question 327

In a change management protocol, what should be the first step after proposing a new change to the security infrastructure?

- A) Directly implementing the change to see real-time effects and adjustments.
- B) Update the organization's security policy to include the proposed change.
- C) Send an email notification about the change to all employees.
- D) Conducting a risk assessment to evaluate potential impacts of the change.

Correct Answer: D

Explanation: Conducting a risk assessment as the first step after proposing a new change is essential to evaluate the potential impacts of the change on the existing security infrastructure. This allows the organization to identify risks and devise mitigation strategies, ensuring that changes enhance security without introducing new vulnerabilities.

Question 328

Fill in the blank: A comprehensive change management strategy ensures that all changes are _____ before implementation.

- A) communicated in a general meeting without detailed documentation.

- B) documented in an internal newsletter for informational purposes.
- C) approved automatically by senior IT management.
- D) thoroughly reviewed and tested.

Correct Answer: D

Explanation: Ensuring that all changes are thoroughly reviewed and tested before implementation is a cornerstone of effective change management. This practice prevents issues from going live, which could otherwise result in security breaches or failures, thus safeguarding the integrity and security of IT systems.

Question 329

The IT department wants to replace its firewall with a more advanced model. What is a critical step in the change management process for this action?

- A) Purchase the most expensive firewall available to guarantee security.
- B) Conduct a survey to see if users prefer the features of the new firewall.
- C) Upgrade all associated network equipment at the same time as the firewall.
- D) Develop a rollback plan to revert back to the old firewall if the new model fails.

Correct Answer: D

Explanation: Developing a rollback plan in case the new firewall does not function as expected or introduces new issues is a critical step in the change management process. This plan ensures that the organization can quickly revert to a stable state without compromising network security, providing a safety net during transitions.

Question 330

During a change review meeting, it was noted that a recent change led to increased security vulnerabilities. What is the immediate action to take under change management principles?

- A) Increase the security settings to the maximum level without reviewing the change.
- B) Scale back all recent changes to default settings without analysis.
- C) Conduct a post-implementation review to identify and mitigate the vulnerabilities.
- D) Ignore the issues unless further problems manifest during normal operations.

Correct Answer: C

Explanation: Conducting a post-implementation review after observing that a change increased security vulnerabilities is crucial. This review helps to identify what went wrong and why, allowing the organization to implement corrective actions effectively and refine the change management process to prevent future occurrences.

Question 331

What is the primary goal of configuration management in cybersecurity?

- A) To increase the operational speed of IT systems by optimizing the configuration settings.
- B) To maintain the security and stability of systems by managing changes in a controlled manner.
- C) To facilitate easier troubleshooting by standardizing configurations across all devices.
- D) To reduce the cost of IT maintenance by automating system updates and patches.

Correct Answer: B

Explanation: The primary goal of configuration management in cybersecurity is to maintain the security and stability of systems by managing changes in a controlled manner. This involves careful documentation, approval, and monitoring of changes to prevent unauthorized modifications that could compromise system integrity.

Question 332

Which configuration management practice ensures that changes are tracked and reversible?

- A) Disabling change logs to speed up the configuration process.
- B) Implementing version control systems for all configuration files.
- C) Relying solely on manual tracking of configuration changes by IT staff.
- D) Using proprietary software that does not support export or backup of configuration data.

Correct Answer: B

Explanation: Implementing version control systems for configuration files is a critical practice within configuration management. It ensures that all changes are tracked, versioned, and reversible, which allows for easy backtracking to previous configurations if a new change introduces issues or vulnerabilities.

Question 333

Fill in the blank: Regular configuration audits are critical because they ensure that all systems _____ to the organization's security policies.

- A) are updated periodically.
- B) can be modified by users as needed.
- C) comply consistently.
- D) remain unchanged unless problems occur.

Correct Answer: C

Explanation: Regular configuration audits are essential to ensure that all systems comply consistently with the organization's security policies. These audits help to identify discrepancies or deviations from expected configurations that could lead to security vulnerabilities.

Question 334

An organization decides to update its server configurations to enhance security. What is the first step according to best practices in configuration management?

- A) Immediately apply the updates to all servers without prior testing.
- B) Skip backup and directly overwrite old configurations with new settings.
- C) Create a backup of current configurations before applying any changes.
- D) Conduct a cost-benefit analysis to determine if the updates are financially justifiable.

Correct Answer: C

Explanation: Creating a backup of current configurations before applying any changes is a fundamental first step in the configuration management process. This precaution ensures that the organization can restore to a known, secure state if updates result in unexpected issues or failures.

Question 335

A security breach was traced back to a misconfiguration in the network. What should be the initial response according to configuration management principles?

- A) Review the change logs to identify the unauthorized or incorrect configuration.
- B) Reset all configurations to default settings to eliminate any misconfigurations.
- C) Increase network monitoring to detect any further anomalies immediately.
- D) Deploy additional firewall rules as a preventive measure against similar breaches.

Correct Answer: A

Explanation: Reviewing the change logs to identify unauthorized or incorrect configurations is the initial response recommended after a security breach traced back to a misconfiguration. This review helps pinpoint the exact nature and origin of the misconfiguration, facilitating targeted remediation and preventing recurrence of similar issues.

Question 336

What is the most critical reason for implementing a regular patch management process?

- A) To address security vulnerabilities before they can be exploited by attackers.
- B) To enhance the functionality of software with new features and improvements.
- C) To ensure compliance with international standards and regulations.
- D) To optimize the IT infrastructure's performance and efficiency.

Correct Answer: A

Explanation: Implementing a regular patch management process is critical for addressing security vulnerabilities promptly. This practice is essential for maintaining the security of systems and data by ensuring that vulnerabilities are patched before they can be exploited by attackers, thereby reducing the window of opportunity for potential breaches.

Question 337

Which strategy ensures that patches do not disrupt system functionality?

- A) Deploying patches during off-peak hours to minimize impact on users.
- B) Applying patches as soon as they are released without prior testing.
- C) Allowing automatic updates without any oversight or review process.
- D) Testing patches in a controlled environment prior to full deployment.

Correct Answer: D

Explanation: Testing patches in a controlled environment before full deployment is a prudent strategy to ensure that they do not disrupt system functionality. This step allows IT teams to identify and resolve any issues caused by the patch in a limited and manageable context, thus preventing widespread problems across the organization's IT infrastructure.

Question 338

Fill in the blank: Patch management policies should mandate that patches be _____ before widespread deployment.

- A) directly approved by top management.
- B) thoroughly tested.
- C) signed off by the security compliance officer.
- D) reviewed in a weekly IT department meeting.

Correct Answer: B

Explanation: Mandating that patches be thoroughly tested before widespread deployment helps to avoid introducing new issues into production environments. This testing confirms the patch's compatibility and effectiveness in addressing the intended security vulnerabilities without adverse effects on system stability and performance.

Question 339

A new critical security patch is released. What is the first action to take under best practices in patch management?

- A) Announce the availability of the patch to all users and recommend manual updates.
- B) Download and deploy the patch immediately to all systems.
- C) Wait for others in the industry to apply the patch and report on its efficacy.
- D) Assess the patch for relevance and urgency in relation to your environment.

Correct Answer: D

Explanation: Assessing a patch for relevance and urgency before deployment ensures that the organization prioritizes patches based on the specific needs and potential risks to its environment. This assessment guides the appropriate allocation of resources and scheduling, enhancing the efficiency and effectiveness of the patch management process.

Question 340
After deploying a patch, several systems experience performance issues. What is the recommended patch management response?

- A) Ignore the issues unless they escalate to critical system failures.
- B) Review the deployment process and system logs to identify the cause of the issues.
- C) Increase network bandwidth to accommodate the extra load from the patch.
- D) Roll back the patch immediately on all systems to avoid further disruptions.

Correct Answer: B

Explanation: Reviewing the deployment process and system logs after encountering performance issues post-patch helps to pinpoint the root cause of the problem. This approach allows for targeted remediation strategies, whether it involves adjusting the deployment process, reconfiguring affected systems, or escalating the issue with the vendor, thus ensuring a systematic resolution to maintain system integrity and performance.

Question 341
What is the fundamental purpose of an incident management workflow in cybersecurity?

- A) To create a detailed report for each incident for insurance purposes only.
- B) To provide a template for legal compliance without necessarily stopping the incident.
- C) To ensure that all security incidents are escalated to senior management immediately.
- D) To systematically manage the process of identifying, analyzing, and responding to security incidents.

Correct Answer: D

Explanation: The fundamental purpose of an incident management workflow in cybersecurity is to manage the process of identifying, analyzing, and responding to security incidents systematically. This ensures that incidents are handled efficiently and effectively, minimizing damage and restoring normal operations as quickly as possible.

Question 342

Which step is critical immediately following the detection of a security incident?

- A) Launch a full backup of all systems to preserve current data state.
- B) Notify all users within the organization about the details of the incident.
- C) Assess the financial implications of the incident before taking any actions.
- D) Contain the incident to prevent further damage or data loss.

Correct Answer: D

Explanation: Containing the incident immediately after detection is critical to prevent further damage or data loss. This step limits the spread of the incident and secures the environment to facilitate a thorough investigation and recovery, thereby protecting organizational assets and reducing recovery time and costs.

Question 343

Fill in the blank: A robust incident management system must ensure that all incidents are _____ to facilitate effective response and recovery.

- A) only communicated to the IT department for internal tracking.
- B) ignored until a similar incident occurs to confirm a pattern.
- C) shared publicly to maintain transparency with customers.
- D) quickly and accurately documented.

Correct Answer: D

Explanation: Ensuring that all incidents are quickly and accurately documented is crucial for a robust incident management system. Documentation supports effective response and recovery by providing detailed incident logs that help in understanding the breach's nature and scope, thus guiding the response team in implementing the most appropriate recovery measures.

Question 344

Upon discovering an unauthorized data breach, what is the first action an incident response team should take?

- A) Assess the scope and impact of the breach to prioritize response actions.
- B) Shut down the entire network to ensure no further data can be compromised.
- C) Contact external cybersecurity consultants to manage the breach.
- D) Immediately inform the media to control the narrative around the breach.

Correct Answer: A

Explanation: Assessing the scope and impact of a breach as the first action helps to prioritize response actions effectively. This assessment provides critical information on the extent of the breach and the data or systems affected, which is essential for focusing resources and efforts where they are most needed to mitigate the breach's effects.

Question 345

After resolving a security incident, what is an essential activity to improve future response efforts?

- A) Implement a mandatory password reset for all users regardless of impact.
- B) Redesign the entire network infrastructure to enhance security.
- C) Conduct a post-incident review to identify lessons learned and update protocols.
- D) Conduct an employee satisfaction survey to gauge the impact of the incident.

Correct Answer: C

Explanation: Conducting a post-incident review after resolving a security incident is essential for improving future response efforts. This review helps identify what went well and what didn't during the incident response, providing valuable insights that can be used to strengthen the incident response plan and enhance the overall security posture.

Question 346

Which of the following best describes the role of a threat intelligence service within a corporate security operations center?

- A) It enables proactive detection and mitigation of security threats by analyzing trends and patterns from various data sources.
- B) It mainly functions to log and document all security breaches without actively preventing future incidents.
- C) It focuses solely on hardware upgrades to improve network security and resilience against attacks.
- D) It supports compliance and regulatory reporting requirements by documenting threats and mitigation actions.

Correct Answer: A

Explanation: Proactive threat detection and mitigation form the backbone of effective security operations centers. By leveraging data from diverse sources, threat intelligence services can anticipate and neutralize threats before they materialize, ensuring robust defense mechanisms are continuously updated and relevant.

Question 347

What is the primary function of Cyber Threat Intelligence (CTI) in enhancing an organization's security posture?

- A) It enables real-time response to incidents by deploying defensive measures against detected threats.
- B) It identifies potential security threats and vulnerabilities to prevent them from being exploited.
- C) It offers cryptographic measures to secure data transmissions against potential eavesdropping or tampering.
- D) It provides a periodic audit of network activities and assesses compliance with security policies.

Correct Answer: B

Explanation: Cyber Threat Intelligence plays a crucial role by pinpointing potential threats and highlighting vulnerabilities. This preemptive knowledge allows organizations to devise strategic defenses that safeguard critical assets before any exploitation can occur.

Question 348

Fill in the blank: _____ platforms automate the collection and analysis of threat data to help predict future attacks.

- A) Network behavior anomaly detection
- B) Threat intelligence and analysis
- C) Security information and event management
- D) Automated security response systems

Correct Answer: B

Explanation: Threat intelligence and analysis platforms streamline the handling of vast amounts of data concerning emerging threats. This automation supports predictive capabilities, making it possible for organizations to preemptively adjust their security measures in anticipation of possible attacks.

Question 349

During a simulated incident response exercise, a security analyst receives an alert that an external IP known for distributing malware is attempting to communicate with a server in the DMZ. What should be the initial step in the threat intelligence process?

- A) Conduct a forensic analysis on the server to determine the extent of any breach or data exfiltration.
- B) Isolate the affected server and remove it from the network to prevent further infection.
- C) Update firewall rules to block traffic from the suspicious IP immediately.
- D) Verify the reliability of the threat data by comparing it with known threat databases.

Correct Answer: D

Explanation: In the scenario of receiving alerts about potential malicious activity, verifying the threat data's reliability ensures that the response is appropriate and measured. Reference against known databases confirms if the alert warrants further action, optimizing resource allocation during incident responses.

Question 350

An IT security team is reviewing the effectiveness of their newly implemented threat intelligence tools. After noticing a decrease in incident response times, what should be the next step in ensuring continuous improvement in threat detection?

- A) Assess whether the changes in the tools or operational procedures contributed to the improvement.
- B) Implement stricter access controls and review existing security policies for effectiveness.
- C) Run a series of penetration tests to identify new vulnerabilities introduced by the tool.
- D) Conduct a cost-benefit analysis of the intelligence tools to decide on further investments or changes.

Correct Answer: A

Explanation: After observing improved incident response times due to the implementation of threat intelligence tools, it's vital to evaluate the specific impacts of these tools. This assessment helps determine the exact elements that contributed to the efficiency gains, which is essential for continuous refinement of security protocols.

Question 351

Which encryption algorithm is best suited for securing real-time communication systems such as VoIP?

- A) Advanced Encryption Standard (AES)
- B) Triple Data Encryption Standard (3DES)
- C) Rivest-Shamir-Adleman (RSA)
- D) Elliptic Curve Cryptography (ECC)

Correct Answer: A

Explanation: Advanced Encryption Standard (AES) is widely recognized for its efficiency in securing real-time communication systems, such as VoIP, due to its speed and strong encryption capabilities. Its ability to encrypt large data streams quickly makes it ideal for applications where performance is critical.

Question 352

What is the main advantage of symmetric encryption over asymmetric encryption when used in large data transfers?

- A) It provides a higher level of security for public key encryption.
- B) It ensures data integrity by using digital signatures along with the encryption process.
- C) It provides stronger encryption by combining two keys, making the encryption harder to break.
- D) It requires lower computational power, making it faster for bulk data encryption.

Correct Answer: D

Explanation: Symmetric encryption algorithms like AES are typically faster and require less computational power than asymmetric algorithms. This makes them especially advantageous when encrypting large amounts of data, as they can provide strong security without introducing significant performance overhead.

Question 353

Fill in the blank: _____ is commonly used to encrypt wireless network traffic and relies on a pre-shared key for authentication.

- A) Counter Mode with Cipher Block Chaining-Message Authentication Code Protocol (CCMP)
- B) Wired Equivalent Privacy (WEP)
- C) WPA2 (Wi-Fi Protected Access 2)
- D) Temporal Key Integrity Protocol (TKIP)

Correct Answer: C

Explanation: WPA2 is a robust encryption standard used to secure wireless networks. It utilizes a pre-shared key (PSK) for authentication, ensuring that only authorized devices can connect to the network. This combination of strong encryption and secure key management is effective in protecting wireless communication.

Question 354

A security consultant is tasked with securing data transmissions between two corporate offices. The offices are located in different regions and the data includes sensitive financial records. The consultant recommends using a combination of asymmetric encryption for key exchange and symmetric encryption for the data itself. What encryption method should be used for data transmission?

- A) Utilize Elliptic Curve Cryptography (ECC) for both key exchange and encrypting the data.
- B) Use Advanced Encryption Standard (AES) for secure and efficient data transmission.
- C) Implement RSA encryption for secure key exchange and data transmission.
- D) Employ Triple DES (3DES) for its compatibility with legacy systems while maintaining data confidentiality.

Correct Answer: B

Explanation: In scenarios involving data transmission across geographically dispersed offices, using asymmetric encryption for secure key exchange combined with symmetric encryption (AES) for the actual data ensures both security and performance. AES is chosen for data transmission because it offers a strong balance between security and speed, essential for sensitive financial records.

Question 355

A company's database containing customer records was encrypted using AES-256 encryption. An attacker managed to obtain access to the encrypted files, but does not possess the key. The attacker attempts to use brute force to decrypt the database. How effective is this attack against AES-256 encryption?

- A) AES-256 is vulnerable to brute force attacks only if the attacker uses a quantum computer.
- B) Brute force attacks against AES-256 are computationally infeasible within a realistic timeframe.
- C) Brute force attacks can successfully decrypt AES-256 if sufficient time and resources are available.
- D) Brute force attempts against AES-256 can be mitigated with additional layers of security like hashing.

Correct Answer: B

Explanation: AES-256 is highly resistant to brute force attacks due to its large key size, making it computationally infeasible to crack within any reasonable timeframe using current technology. Even with significant resources, an attacker would require an impractical amount of time to try all possible keys, rendering brute force ineffective against

AES-256.

Question 356
Which network security measure is designed to detect and prevent unauthorized access attempts on internal networks?

- A) Network Address Translation (NAT)
- B) Data Loss Prevention (DLP)
- C) Intrusion Prevention System (IPS)
- D) Stateful Firewall

Correct Answer: C

Explanation: An Intrusion Prevention System (IPS) actively monitors network traffic and automatically takes action to prevent unauthorized access attempts. Unlike passive systems, IPS can block malicious activity before it affects the network, making it an essential tool for securing internal networks.

Question 357
What is the advantage of implementing Network Access Control (NAC) in an organization's network security strategy?

- A) It reduces the likelihood of insider threats by limiting access to internal resources.
- B) It enforces security policies by authenticating devices before granting network access.
- C) It ensures that all data transmissions are encrypted, protecting sensitive data in transit.
- D) It improves performance by allowing only authorized devices to connect, reducing congestion.

Correct Answer: B

Explanation: Network Access Control (NAC) enforces security by ensuring that only authorized and authenticated devices can access the network. This helps in preventing rogue devices from connecting to the internal network, thereby reducing potential attack vectors and maintaining overall network security.

Question 358

Fill in the blank: _____ is used to create secure communication tunnels between remote users and the organization's internal network.

- A) Virtual Private Network (VPN)
- B) Firewall
- C) Proxy Server
- D) Intrusion Detection System (IDS)

Correct Answer: A

Explanation: Virtual Private Network (VPN) technology provides secure, encrypted tunnels for communication between remote users or offices and the internal network. It ensures data confidentiality and integrity, making it a common solution for securing communications over untrusted networks, such as the internet.

Question 359

An IT administrator is responsible for securing a corporate network that connects multiple branch offices via the internet. To protect data in transit and ensure secure communication between these offices, which security method should be applied?

- A) Enable Network Address Translation (NAT) to provide security by masking internal IP addresses.
- B) Apply Virtual Private Network (VPN) encryption for secure and private communication between offices.
- C) Deploy a proxy server to manage and secure communication between different office

locations.
- D) Use a stateful firewall to monitor traffic and filter connections between branch offices.

Correct Answer: B

Explanation: When securing communication between geographically separated offices, a VPN is the most appropriate solution. It creates encrypted communication tunnels, ensuring that sensitive data transmitted between locations remains secure from interception or tampering.

Question 360

A company's external-facing web server has been experiencing a high number of malicious traffic attempts originating from various IP addresses. The network security team wants to block these attempts without affecting legitimate traffic. What is the most efficient way to mitigate these threats?

- A) Use a Deep Packet Inspection system to analyze traffic patterns and block malicious content.
- B) Implement application-layer filtering to block attacks based on specific application behaviors.
- C) Implement geolocation-based IP filtering to block traffic from specific regions.
- D) Use a Web Application Firewall (WAF) to block traffic based on content inspection and predefined rules.

Correct Answer: C

Explanation: Geolocation-based IP filtering allows the security team to block traffic originating from specific regions or countries known for generating malicious activity. This method helps reduce the volume of malicious traffic while maintaining legitimate access from trusted regions, ensuring the web server's performance remains unaffected.

Question 361

Which cloud security technology is designed to monitor and enforce security policies across multiple cloud environments, including hybrid setups?

- A) Virtual Private Cloud (VPC)
- B) Security Information and Event Management (SIEM)
- C) Firewall as a Service (FWaaS)
- D) Cloud Access Security Broker (CASB)

Correct Answer: D

Explanation: A Cloud Access Security Broker (CASB) helps secure cloud environments by acting as a policy enforcement point between users and cloud services. It ensures that security policies are consistently applied across multiple cloud environments, including hybrid configurations, providing centralized control and monitoring of cloud usage.

Question 362

What is the advantage of encrypting data at rest in cloud environments compared to only encrypting data in transit?

- A) It protects against unauthorized access to stored data, even if the storage system is compromised.
- B) It only focuses on encrypting communications but leaves the stored data vulnerable to unauthorized access.
- C) It guarantees that data integrity is maintained while the data is being accessed over the network.
- D) It helps detect unauthorized access by focusing on traffic encryption alone without protecting stored data.

Correct Answer: A

Explanation: Encrypting data at rest provides an additional layer of security for sensitive information stored in cloud environments. Even if a malicious actor gains unauthorized access to the storage system, they cannot read the data without the encryption keys. This helps ensure the confidentiality of data even when it is not actively being transmitted.

Question 363

Fill in the blank: _____ is a security measure that ensures user access to cloud services is granted based on their roles within the organization.

- A) Role-Based Access Control (RBAC)
- B) Public Key Infrastructure (PKI)
- C) Multifactor Authentication (MFA)
- D) Identity and Access Management (IAM)

Correct Answer: A

Explanation: Role-Based Access Control (RBAC) ensures that access to cloud resources is granted based on the roles of individual users within the organization. This reduces the risk of unauthorized access by limiting permissions to only what each user requires to perform their duties, enhancing the overall security of cloud environments.

Question 364

A company has recently migrated its internal database to a cloud provider. To maintain compliance with data privacy regulations, the organization needs to ensure that no unauthorized personnel can access sensitive data. What security control should the organization implement to secure the cloud environment?

- A) Use encryption for data in transit to ensure security during the transmission process.
- B) Apply strict network segmentation and monitoring to minimize unauthorized access in the cloud.
- C) Ensure security configurations meet industry standards by applying custom rules across the cloud infrastructure.
- D) Implement encryption and access control measures to secure data within the cloud environment.

Correct Answer: D

Explanation: To secure cloud environments and maintain compliance with data privacy regulations, encryption should be used to protect sensitive information. Access control measures must also be implemented to ensure only authorized personnel can view or modify the data. Together, these controls provide robust security in cloud-based systems.

Question 365

A financial services firm utilizes multiple cloud platforms to store customer data. Recently, the firm experienced a data breach involving one of its third-party cloud services. The security team needs to audit the incident and ensure proper security configurations are in place across all cloud platforms. What solution would provide centralized visibility and control over the security configurations of these platforms?

- A) Apply a Virtual Private Cloud (VPC) to isolate critical cloud services from external threats.
- B) Employ an Endpoint Detection and Response (EDR) system to secure endpoints connected to cloud platforms.
- C) Use an Intrusion Detection System (IDS) to identify potential threats across cloud environments.
- D) Utilize a Cloud Access Security Broker (CASB) to manage security policies and monitor all cloud services.

Correct Answer: D

Explanation: A Cloud Access Security Broker (CASB) provides centralized visibility into the security configurations of multiple cloud platforms, helping organizations ensure compliance and manage security risks. By monitoring and enforcing security policies across different cloud environments, CASBs help detect and prevent data breaches like the one described in this scenario.

Question 366

Which endpoint security solution is designed to monitor and detect suspicious behavior on end-user devices, preventing malware infections and unauthorized activities?

- A) Application whitelisting software
- B) Mobile Device Management (MDM)
- C) Antivirus with behavioral detection
- D) Endpoint Detection and Response (EDR)

Correct Answer: D

Explanation: Endpoint Detection and Response (EDR) solutions are designed to continuously monitor end-user devices, detecting suspicious behavior and preventing malware infections in real time. EDR tools also allow for swift remediation, enabling security teams to respond effectively to potential threats before they cause significant damage.

Question 367

What is the primary benefit of deploying an endpoint detection and response (EDR) solution across all company devices?

- A) It ensures that devices remain compliant with security policies, preventing unauthorized modifications.
- B) It provides real-time visibility into endpoint activities and automates responses to potential threats.
- C) It secures sensitive data stored on endpoints, ensuring its integrity and confidentiality.
- D) It minimizes the risk of insider threats by controlling and monitoring device access points.

Correct Answer: B

Explanation: Deploying endpoint detection and response (EDR) solutions across company devices allows security teams to monitor activities on all endpoints in real time. This capability enhances threat detection by identifying unusual behavior and responding automatically, reducing the potential impact of malware or unauthorized access.

Question 368

Fill in the blank: _____ is a security measure that enforces device encryption, ensuring data protection on lost or stolen end-user devices.

- A) Public Key Infrastructure (PKI)
- B) Virtual Private Network (VPN)
- C) Full Disk Encryption (FDE)
- D) Identity and Access Management (IAM)

Correct Answer: C

Explanation: Full Disk Encryption (FDE) ensures that all data stored on end-user devices remains encrypted, protecting sensitive information if the device is lost or stolen. Even if an attacker gains physical access to the device, they cannot retrieve the encrypted data without the appropriate decryption key, providing a strong layer of protection.

Question 369

A system administrator is tasked with implementing endpoint security measures on all company laptops to safeguard sensitive data. The company requires solutions that can prevent unauthorized access, monitor device activity, and encrypt local data. Which security control should the administrator prioritize first to protect end-user devices effectively?

- A) Implement endpoint detection and response (EDR) software to monitor devices and detect malicious activities.
- B) Enforce strict application whitelisting policies to allow only authorized software on devices.
- C) Apply mobile device management (MDM) and device encryption policies to secure mobile devices.
- D) Deploy multifactor authentication (MFA) and identity management systems to control access.

Correct Answer: A

Explanation: In a scenario where endpoint security must be implemented on company laptops, starting with EDR software is critical. EDR tools provide comprehensive monitoring and threat detection, helping to safeguard sensitive data, prevent unauthorized access, and mitigate the risk of malware infections on end-user devices.

Question 370

A financial institution has noticed an increase in phishing attacks targeting its employees. Several compromised endpoints have been detected as a result. The security team needs to ensure all end-user devices are protected and capable of detecting future attacks. What endpoint security solution should the institution implement to defend against phishing and other malware threats?

- A) Deploy advanced anti-malware and endpoint detection and response (EDR) tools to secure all devices.
- B) Utilize firewall and intrusion detection systems to block unauthorized access and external threats.
- C) Install device encryption and a secure email gateway to prevent phishing attempts.
- D) Implement phishing filters and regular employee security awareness training to reduce the threat.

Correct Answer: A

Explanation: Advanced anti-malware and endpoint detection and response (EDR) tools are essential for securing end-user devices against phishing attacks and other malware threats. By providing continuous monitoring and real-time threat detection, these tools help protect the institution from future phishing attempts and quickly respond to any new threats.

Which Mobile Device Management (MDM) feature is responsible for ensuring that all corporate mobile devices are compliant with the organization's security policies before allowing access to sensitive data?

- A) Encryption enforcement
- B) Application whitelisting
- C) Device access logging
- D) Device compliance checks

Correct Answer: D

Explanation: Device compliance checks ensure that mobile devices meet the organization's security standards before they are granted access to sensitive corporate resources. This feature enforces security policies such as encryption, password protection, and app restrictions, reducing the risk of data breaches by ensuring that only compliant devices can access the network.

Question 372

What is the main benefit of using a Mobile Device Management (MDM) system to enforce remote wipe functionality on lost or stolen devices?

- A) It helps locate lost devices through GPS tracking, allowing the user to recover the device before any data breach occurs.
- B) It ensures that devices remain locked, preventing unauthorized users from attempting to access stored data.
- C) It prevents malware infections by ensuring that lost devices cannot access external networks.
- D) It protects sensitive data by allowing the IT department to erase all data remotely, preventing unauthorized access.

Correct Answer: D

Explanation: Remote wipe functionality is a critical feature provided by MDM systems, allowing IT administrators to erase all data on lost or stolen devices. This ensures that sensitive corporate information is not accessible to unauthorized individuals if the device is lost, significantly reducing the risk of data breaches.

Question 373

Fill in the blank: _____ is a feature of Mobile Device Management (MDM) that separates personal and work data on the same device, ensuring data security for corporate information.

- A) Geofencing
- B) Encryption
- C) Data loss prevention (DLP)
- D) Containerization

Correct Answer: D

Explanation: Containerization within MDM solutions creates a secure partition between personal and corporate data on mobile devices. This separation ensures that corporate data is protected from unauthorized access, even if the device is used for personal activities, thereby maintaining data security without infringing on the user's personal information.

Question 374

A company issues smartphones to all its sales representatives to access corporate email, customer databases, and other sensitive data while traveling. To ensure the security of these mobile assets, the IT department needs to apply security controls such as encryption, app restrictions, and geofencing. Which Mobile Device Management (MDM) feature should the IT team use to enforce these controls?

- A) Apply multifactor authentication and role-based access control to limit data access on mobile devices.
- B) Enforce data loss prevention policies to block unauthorized data transfers from the mobile devices.
- C) Set up encryption policies to ensure that all data stored on mobile devices is secure

from unauthorized access.
- D) Use device compliance checks and application control to enforce security policies and restrictions on the devices.

Correct Answer: D

Explanation: Device compliance checks and application control features allow IT teams to enforce specific security policies, such as encryption and app restrictions, across mobile devices. These controls ensure that corporate devices are securely configured and that employees can only access approved applications and data.

Question 375

An enterprise organization has experienced several incidents where mobile devices were lost, potentially exposing sensitive customer data. The security team has implemented an MDM solution to address this risk. What security measure should the MDM enforce to prevent data breaches if a device is lost?

- A) Enable encryption and enforce remote wipe on lost devices to secure sensitive data and prevent unauthorized access.
- B) Implement geofencing to disable device functionality outside of approved geographic locations.
- C) Use multifactor authentication to ensure only authorized users can access the device in case of theft.
- D) Require VPN usage for secure communications between the device and corporate networks to prevent data interception.

Correct Answer: A

Explanation: Enforcing encryption and remote wipe through an MDM solution ensures that if a mobile device is lost or stolen, the data stored on the device remains secure. Encryption makes the data unreadable without the decryption key, and remote wipe allows the IT team to erase all sensitive information, preventing unauthorized access or data exposure.

Question 376

What is the key advantage of using Security Information and Event Management (SIEM) systems to detect security threats in an enterprise environment?

- A) It prevents all types of attacks by automatically blocking suspicious traffic based on predefined security policies.
- B) It stores all security logs in a centralized location for later review, enabling historical analysis of potential attacks.
- C) It automates the response to detected threats by isolating affected endpoints to prevent further compromise.
- D) It centralizes security data collection and provides real-time analysis of security events from multiple sources.

Correct Answer: D

Explanation: SIEM systems centralize security event data collection from multiple sources, providing real-time visibility and analysis of potential security threats. This allows security teams to detect suspicious activity across the enterprise in real time, helping them respond to incidents quickly and efficiently.

Question 377

Which of the following is a critical function of SIEM systems that allows for correlating events from multiple sources to identify potential security incidents?

- A) Event normalization
- B) Event correlation
- C) Log aggregation
- D) Threat intelligence integration

Correct Answer: B

Explanation: Event correlation is a key function of SIEM systems that enables the system to detect patterns and relationships between different security events across various devices and applications. By correlating these events, SIEM systems can identify complex security incidents that might otherwise go unnoticed if each event were analyzed in isolation.

Question 378

Fill in the blank: _____ is the process within SIEM systems that involves analyzing and categorizing security events to prioritize incidents based on risk.

- A) Data classification
- B) Automated reporting
- C) Real-time monitoring
- D) Event prioritization

Correct Answer: D

Explanation: Event prioritization within SIEM systems helps security teams focus on the most critical incidents by assigning a risk score to each event. This ensures that security professionals can address high-priority incidents first, reducing the potential for harm to the organization's systems and data.

Question 379

An enterprise organization has implemented a SIEM system to monitor network activity across multiple locations. The security team is noticing several alerts triggered by normal employee behavior, causing alert fatigue. How should the team adjust the SIEM system to ensure it generates alerts only for legitimate threats?

- A) Tune the SIEM system to reduce false positives and focus on specific behavioral patterns that indicate threats.
- B) Apply network segmentation and stricter access control policies to reduce the risk of unauthorized access.
- C) Deploy a more robust intrusion detection system to filter out benign network activity.
- D) Increase the threshold for event severity to minimize the number of alerts generated by normal user behavior.

Correct Answer: A

Explanation: Tuning a SIEM system is essential to reduce false positives, which occur when benign activity triggers alerts. By fine-tuning the system to focus on specific threat patterns and eliminating irrelevant alerts, security teams can reduce alert fatigue and focus on legitimate threats.

Question 380

A large retail company experiences a data breach involving multiple compromised endpoints across different stores. The SIEM system logs numerous events, including unusual login attempts and file transfers. What should be the first step for the security team in analyzing these events to understand the breach?

- A) Filter out non-critical events and focus on anomalies related to compromised credentials.
- B) Review correlated events within the SIEM system to identify patterns that point to the origin of the breach.
- C) Analyze the raw logs manually to determine which events require immediate action.
- D) Investigate individual alerts to track the origin and cause of each suspicious activity.

Correct Answer: B

Explanation: In the event of a breach involving multiple compromised endpoints, the security team should first review correlated events in the SIEM system. Correlation allows the team to identify related activities, such as unusual login attempts or unauthorized file transfers, which can help trace the origin and scope of the breach.

Question 381

Which Identity and Access Management (IAM) feature ensures that employees only have the minimum level of access required to perform their job functions?

- A) User provisioning
- B) Role-based access control
- C) Least privilege access
- D) Privileged access management

Correct Answer: C

Explanation: Least privilege access is a critical IAM feature that limits user permissions to only what is necessary for their role. This reduces the attack surface by preventing unauthorized access to sensitive systems, even if a user's account is compromised.

Question 382

What is the benefit of using multifactor authentication (MFA) as part of an IAM strategy for securing access to sensitive systems?

- A) It eliminates the need for passwords, allowing employees to access systems using biometric verification.
- B) It adds an extra layer of security by requiring multiple factors to verify a user's identity before granting access.
- C) It provides a single sign-on solution for multiple services, making it easier to manage user credentials.
- D) It simplifies the login process by automatically detecting and allowing recognized devices to access systems.

Correct Answer: B

Explanation: Multifactor authentication (MFA) enhances security by requiring users to provide two or more verification methods, such as a password and a biometric scan, before gaining access. This greatly reduces the likelihood of unauthorized access, as it makes it harder for attackers to bypass the authentication process.

Question 383

Fill in the blank: _____ is a security concept within IAM that enforces automatic deactivation of access privileges after a predetermined period of inactivity.

- A) Access recertification
- B) User inactivity monitoring
- C) Time-based access control
- D) Role delegation

Correct Answer: A

Explanation: Access recertification involves periodically reviewing user access rights and revoking any permissions that are no longer necessary. This process ensures that inactive accounts or users who have changed roles do not retain access to systems they no longer need, which reduces potential security risks.

Question 384

A company has implemented a role-based access control (RBAC) system as part of its IAM strategy. During an internal audit, it was discovered that several employees have access to systems they do not require for their roles. What should the security team do to resolve this issue and ensure compliance with the least privilege principle?

- A) Reassess and update user roles and permissions to align with the least privilege principle.
- B) Apply multifactor authentication to secure access to systems with sensitive information.
- C) Remove all unnecessary user accounts and enforce strong password policies across the organization.
- D) Implement network segmentation to prevent unauthorized access to sensitive systems.

Correct Answer: A

Explanation: To resolve the issue of employees having unnecessary access, the security team should reassess and update user roles. By realigning permissions with the least privilege principle, the team can ensure that employees have access only to the systems they require for their specific roles, improving both security and compliance.

Question 385

A global organization uses an IAM system to manage access across multiple locations. Recently, employees have reported difficulty accessing systems during international business trips due to geographical restrictions imposed by the IAM system. What solution should the security team implement to provide secure access while ensuring compliance with company policies?

- A) Introduce geolocation-based login permissions that allow access only from specific regions.
- B) Use conditional access policies to allow secure access based on risk factors such as location and device.
- C) Disable geographical restrictions and implement VPNs for secure remote access.
- D) Disable geographic restrictions entirely to provide unrestricted global access.

Correct Answer: B

Explanation: Conditional access policies allow the IAM system to evaluate factors such as user location and device type before granting access. This solution provides secure access to users traveling internationally while ensuring that company policies, such as geolocation-based restrictions, are still enforced.

Question 386

Which firewall configuration ensures that incoming traffic is only allowed through specific ports and IP addresses while blocking all other traffic?

- A) Deny by default

- B) Stateful packet filtering
- C) Blocklisting
- D) Allowlisting

Correct Answer: D

Explanation: Allowlisting ensures that only trusted IP addresses and ports are allowed through the firewall, while all other traffic is blocked. This configuration significantly enhances security by minimizing the attack surface and preventing unauthorized access to the network.

Question 387

What is the advantage of using a stateful firewall over a stateless firewall in protecting a corporate network?

- A) It limits traffic by allowing only connections initiated from inside the network, reducing external threats.
- B) It filters traffic based only on static rules, without tracking ongoing connections.
- C) It enhances security by allowing only explicitly permitted traffic and blocking all other traffic.
- D) It tracks the state of active connections and makes decisions based on the context of the traffic.

Correct Answer: D

Explanation: A stateful firewall provides more advanced protection than a stateless one by keeping track of active connections and making decisions based on the context of the traffic flow. This allows it to detect and block suspicious traffic that might otherwise bypass stateless filters.

Question 388

Fill in the blank: _____ is a technique used in firewall management to prevent unauthorized access to internal systems by blocking traffic from specific geographic locations.

- A) Access Control List (ACL)
- B) Geolocation filtering
- C) Deep Packet Inspection (DPI)
- D) Port forwarding

Correct Answer: B

Explanation: Geolocation filtering enables firewall administrators to block traffic originating from specific geographic regions known for malicious activity. This technique is particularly useful in preventing attacks from countries where certain types of cyberattacks are prevalent, reducing the risk of unauthorized access.

Question 389

A network administrator notices unusual traffic patterns that suggest an ongoing attack from multiple external IP addresses. The administrator needs to block these IP addresses without affecting legitimate traffic. What firewall management action should the administrator take to mitigate this threat?

- A) Disable the affected ports and apply stricter network segmentation to contain the attack.
- B) Implement a web application firewall to monitor and filter HTTP traffic.
- C) Block the specific external IP addresses while maintaining normal traffic through allowlisting.
- D) Set up network address translation (NAT) to obscure the internal IP addresses of critical systems.

Correct Answer: C

Explanation: When unusual traffic patterns suggest an attack, blocking specific external IP addresses through allowlisting is an effective firewall management action. This ensures that legitimate traffic from trusted IP addresses can still pass through, while malicious traffic from identified sources is blocked.

Question 390

A large enterprise organization is expanding its network infrastructure by adding new servers. To ensure network security, the firewall rules need to be updated to account for these new servers. What should the network administrator do to ensure the firewall rules are optimized without creating unnecessary security risks?

- A) Implement automated rule updates to quickly adapt to changes in the network infrastructure.
- B) Implement access control lists (ACLs) to limit the traffic to and from the new servers.
- C) Conduct a firewall rule audit to identify unnecessary rules and optimize security for the new servers.
- D) Apply network address translation (NAT) to manage the flow of traffic between the internal and external networks.

Correct Answer: C

Explanation: Conducting a firewall rule audit allows the network administrator to remove outdated or unnecessary rules and adjust the firewall to account for the newly added servers. This ensures that the network remains secure without adding complexity or creating unnecessary risks due to poorly optimized rules.

Question 391

Which feature of an Intrusion Detection System (IDS) allows it to detect potential threats by analyzing known attack patterns in network traffic?

- A) Behavioral monitoring
- B) Rule-based analysis
- C) Signature-based detection
- D) Heuristic analysis

Correct Answer: C

Explanation: Signature-based detection works by comparing traffic patterns against a database of known attack signatures. If a match is found, the IDS generates an alert. This method is effective for detecting well-known threats that follow predictable patterns, such as malware or known exploits.

Question 392

What is the advantage of using a network-based IDS over a host-based IDS for monitoring a corporate network's traffic?

- A) It detects specific traffic behaviors related to known vulnerabilities in each individual system.
- B) It provides detailed analysis of individual hosts but requires additional resources to monitor multiple endpoints.
- C) It monitors all network traffic at key points, detecting threats that affect multiple systems at once.
- D) It captures traffic at the host level, detecting threats that could bypass perimeter defenses.

Correct Answer: C

Explanation: A network-based IDS offers a broader view of traffic by monitoring data flow at key points within the network. This makes it ideal for detecting threats that may affect multiple systems simultaneously. Unlike a host-based IDS, which monitors individual devices, a network-based IDS can capture network-wide anomalies and provide comprehensive coverage.

Question 393

Fill in the blank: _____ is the process in which an IDS identifies normal traffic patterns and flags deviations that could indicate suspicious activity.

- A) Deep Packet Inspection (DPI)
- B) Packet filtering
- C) Stateful inspection
- D) Anomaly detection

Correct Answer: D

Explanation: Anomaly detection involves identifying deviations from established traffic patterns that could indicate suspicious activity. This approach is useful for detecting zero-day attacks and other previously unknown threats, as it does not rely on predefined attack signatures. Anomalies are flagged based on the system's baseline of "normal" traffic.

Question 394

A network administrator notices a high number of false positives from the IDS, causing the security team to spend unnecessary time investigating legitimate traffic. What step should the administrator take to reduce the false positives while maintaining strong security monitoring?

- A) Implement additional security layers, such as firewalls, to filter traffic before it reaches the IDS.
- B) Disable alerts from common applications that generate false positives to focus on critical alerts.
- C) Reconfigure the IDS rules to trigger only on high-priority alerts and lower the sensitivity for normal traffic.
- D) Adjust the IDS to tune out normal traffic patterns and focus on abnormal behaviors that could indicate a threat.

Correct Answer: D

Explanation: To reduce false positives, the IDS should be tuned to recognize normal traffic patterns. By adjusting thresholds or fine-tuning the system's sensitivity to legitimate traffic, the security team can reduce the number of false alerts while still capturing true threats that deviate from typical network behavior.

Question 395

A company is expanding its network to include a large number of IoT devices. The security team is concerned about securing this traffic and ensuring that potential threats are detected. What IDS configuration should the team use to monitor and analyze the increased traffic volume while minimizing the risk of undetected threats?

- A) Use a network-based IDS to monitor traffic from all devices, including IoT, and configure thresholds for detecting anomalies.
- B) Apply machine learning models to distinguish between normal and abnormal traffic across the entire network.
- C) Deploy a hybrid IDS solution that combines network-based and host-based systems to cover all IoT traffic.
- D) Install host-based IDS on individual IoT devices to monitor device-level activity and prevent direct attacks.

Correct Answer: A

Explanation: A network-based IDS is ideal for monitoring the increased traffic generated by IoT devices, as it can analyze traffic across the network in real time. Configuring the IDS to set thresholds for detecting anomalies ensures that the system remains efficient at identifying potential threats without being overwhelmed by the sheer volume of data generated by the new devices.

Question 396

Which application security practice ensures that vulnerabilities are identified and addressed throughout the software development lifecycle (SDLC)?

- A) Code obfuscation techniques
- B) Output encoding strategies

- C) Input validation techniques
- D) Secure coding practices

Correct Answer: D

Explanation: Secure coding practices ensure that potential vulnerabilities are addressed during the development process, reducing the risk of security flaws being introduced into the final product. This proactive approach helps maintain application security throughout the software development lifecycle (SDLC).

Question 397

What is the advantage of using static application security testing (SAST) during the software development process?

- A) It integrates security testing as a final step in the deployment pipeline, ensuring no vulnerabilities exist at the production stage.
- B) It allows the development team to perform runtime testing, capturing security vulnerabilities as they occur in production environments.
- C) It automates security testing after the application has been deployed, enabling real-time feedback on security vulnerabilities.
- D) It identifies vulnerabilities in the code without executing the application, reducing the time needed for fixes.

Correct Answer: D

Explanation: Static application security testing (SAST) identifies vulnerabilities by analyzing the source code before the application is executed. This allows developers to detect and fix security flaws early in the development process, preventing them from reaching production and reducing the time and cost associated with remediation.

Question 398

Fill in the blank: _____ is a security mechanism used in application security to ensure that only authorized users can access specific features or data within an application.

- A) Multifactor authentication (MFA)
- B) Security Information and Event Management (SIEM)
- C) Role-based access control (RBAC)
- D) Deep Packet Inspection (DPI)

Correct Answer: C

Explanation: Role-based access control (RBAC) is a security model that restricts access to application features or data based on the roles of individual users. This ensures that users can only access the resources they are authorized to use, reducing the risk of unauthorized access and data breaches.

Question 399

A development team is building a web application that will handle sensitive financial transactions. To ensure the security of the application, the team wants to integrate security checks directly into their continuous integration/continuous deployment (CI/CD) pipeline. Which tool or practice should the team prioritize to catch vulnerabilities early in the development process?

- A) Implement static application security testing (SAST) within the CI/CD pipeline to catch vulnerabilities early.
- B) Set up a web application firewall (WAF) to protect against external threats targeting the application's dependencies.
- C) Deploy runtime application self-protection (RASP) to monitor the application in real-time for vulnerabilities.
- D) Use dynamic application security testing (DAST) to identify vulnerabilities in the production environment.

Correct Answer: A

Explanation: Integrating static application security testing (SAST) into the CI/CD pipeline allows the development team to catch vulnerabilities early in the development process. By running automated security checks during each build, the team can ensure that security flaws are identified and remediated before the application is deployed.

Question 400

A company has deployed an application in a production environment, but it recently faced a security breach due to unpatched vulnerabilities in third-party libraries. The security team needs to prevent similar breaches in the future. What should the team implement to regularly assess the security of external dependencies in the application?

- A) Install intrusion detection systems (IDS) to monitor and block threats targeting third-party dependencies.
- B) Apply regular vulnerability scanning to identify unpatched software components in the application.
- C) Use software composition analysis (SCA) to continuously monitor and evaluate third-party libraries for known vulnerabilities.
- D) Implement manual penetration testing of third-party libraries to identify risks in production.

Correct Answer: C

Explanation: Software composition analysis (SCA) is a critical practice for identifying and managing vulnerabilities in third-party libraries. By continuously monitoring the application's dependencies, SCA helps the security team detect and address known vulnerabilities, ensuring that external components do not introduce risks into the production environment.

Question 401

Which governance framework is designed specifically for managing IT investments and ensuring alignment with business objectives?

- A) Enterprise Risk Management (ERM)

- B) ISO/IEC 38500
- C) Control Objectives for Information and Related Technology (COBIT)
- D) Information Technology Infrastructure Library (ITIL)

Correct Answer: C

Explanation: COBIT is a comprehensive framework that assists organizations in achieving their objectives for the governance and management of enterprise IT. It bridges the gap between control requirements, technical issues, and business risks.

Question 402

In a cybersecurity context, what governance framework primarily focuses on risk management and information security governance?

- A) National Institute of Standards and Technology (NIST)
- B) IT Infrastructure Library (ITIL)
- C) ISO/IEC 27001
- D) Committee of Sponsoring Organizations (COSO)

Correct Answer: B

Explanation: ITIL focuses specifically on aligning IT services with the needs of the business and emphasizes a process approach to management. It is widely adopted for its detailed practices for IT service management (ITSM) which aim to facilitate the growth and transformation of the business.

Question 403

Fill in the blank: The _____ framework is used globally to guide organizations in effective enterprise governance and management of IT.

- A) Information Technology Infrastructure Library (ITIL)
- B) COBIT
- C) ISO/IEC 27001
- D) Project Management Body of Knowledge (PMBOK)

Correct Answer: B

Explanation: COBIT is recognized globally for its holistic framework and tools that support enterprises in managing and governing their information and technology assets. It provides a structured model that aligns IT efforts with business strategies and manages risks effectively.

Question 404

A company is deploying a new governance framework across its IT department to enhance security posture and compliance. The IT director is evaluating frameworks. Which framework offers a structured approach to aligning IT with business goals while managing risks?

- A) Information Technology Infrastructure Library (ITIL)
- B) Committee of Sponsoring Organizations (COSO)
- C) Control Objectives for Information and Related Technology (COBIT)
- D) Project Management Body of Knowledge (PMBOK)

Correct Answer: C

Explanation: COBIT provides a comprehensive framework that guides enterprises in governing and managing their IT environments. Its principles are designed to ensure that IT investments are aligned with business objectives and managed in a way that optimizes risks and resources.

Question 405

An organization's security team is implementing a governance model that includes compliance with legal and regulatory requirements. They aim to use a framework that incorporates environmental and social governance aspects. What is the most suitable governance framework for this purpose?

- A) Committee of Sponsoring Organizations (COSO)
- B) ISO/IEC 27001
- C) Global Reporting Initiative (GRI)
- D) International Organization for Standardization (ISO) 26000

Correct Answer: D

Explanation: ISO 26000 provides guidance on how businesses and organizations can operate in a socially responsible way, making it suitable for companies looking to incorporate social and environmental governance. It aligns corporate strategy with social responsibility and ethical behavior.

Question 406

What is the first step in a risk management process to secure IT systems?

- A) Develop risk mitigation strategies
- B) Evaluate the effectiveness of existing controls
- C) Identify potential risks
- D) Monitor and review the risk environment

Correct Answer: C

Explanation: Identifying potential risks is the foundational step in any risk management process, as it sets the stage for all subsequent actions, such as analysis, mitigation, and monitoring. Understanding what risks exist is crucial before effective management strategies can be developed.

Question 407

Which method is most effective for quantifying and prioritizing risks in network security?

- A) Risk avoidance
- B) Quantitative risk analysis
- C) Risk transference
- D) Qualitative risk analysis

Correct Answer: B

Explanation: Quantitative risk analysis involves the use of numerical values to estimate the probability and impact of risks, making it an effective tool for prioritizing risks based on their potential severity and likelihood. This method helps organizations allocate resources more efficiently to address the most significant threats.

Question 408

Fill in the blank: In risk management, _____ analysis is crucial for determining the potential impact of identified risks.

- A) Quantitative
- B) Qualitative
- C) Financial
- D) Operational

Correct Answer: A

Explanation: Quantitative analysis in risk management allows for a more precise evaluation of potential impacts by assigning numerical values to the likelihood and consequences of risks. This aids in understanding the severity of risks and informs better decision-making regarding resource allocation and risk treatment.

Question 409

A company's IT department is conducting a risk assessment to address vulnerabilities in its software. What should be their primary focus to effectively manage these risks?

- A) Upgrading hardware to enhance security features
- B) Conducting penetration testing on a regular basis
- C) Increasing cybersecurity awareness among employees
- D) Implementing regular security updates and patch management

Correct Answer: D

Explanation: Implementing regular security updates and patch management is critical for addressing vulnerabilities within software, as these updates often contain fixes for security holes that could be exploited by attackers. Regular updates ensure that the system remains protected against known vulnerabilities.

Question 410

During a security audit, an IT manager discovers an unpatched vulnerability that could allow unauthorized access to confidential data. What should be the first action in the risk mitigation process?

- A) Notify all users about potential data breaches
- B) Assess the risk associated with the vulnerability
- C) Apply for cyber insurance to cover potential losses
- D) Immediately disconnect affected systems from the network

Correct Answer: B

Explanation: Assessing the risk involves analyzing the potential impact and likelihood of the vulnerability being exploited. This is the first step in the risk mitigation process because understanding the severity and exploitability of the vulnerability is essential for determining the appropriate response to reduce the associated risk.

Question 411

What is the primary goal of compliance management in cybersecurity?

- A) Ensuring that IT practices adhere to relevant laws and regulations
- B) Improving customer satisfaction through better service delivery
- C) Maximizing efficiency of IT operations across the company
- D) Minimizing operational costs associated with IT management

Correct Answer: A

Explanation: Compliance management in cybersecurity aims to ensure that IT practices are in line with both legal requirements and industry standards. This is essential not only for avoiding legal penalties but also for maintaining the trust of stakeholders and protecting the organization against cybersecurity threats.

Question 412

Which regulation is specifically focused on protecting personal data within the EU?

- A) Payment Card Industry Data Security Standard (PCI DSS)
- B) Health Insurance Portability and Accountability Act (HIPAA)
- C) Children's Online Privacy Protection Act (COPPA)
- D) General Data Protection Regulation (GDPR)

Correct Answer: D

Explanation: The GDPR is designed to protect personal data and privacy within the European Union and the European Economic Area. It also addresses the transfer of personal data outside the EU and EEA areas, making it critical for companies operating within these regions to comply with its regulations to avoid severe penalties.

Question 413

Fill in the blank: Compliance with _____ is crucial for any U.S. public company to ensure financial data integrity.

- A) Federal Information Security Management Act (FISMA)
- B) California Consumer Privacy Act (CCPA)
- C) General Data Protection Regulation (GDPR)
- D) Sarbanes-Oxley Act (SOX)

Correct Answer: D

Explanation: The Sarbanes-Oxley Act (SOX) requires all publicly traded companies in the U.S. to maintain accurate financial records and implement proper internal controls. Compliance with SOX is crucial for ensuring transparency and protecting investors from accounting errors and fraudulent financial practices.

Question 414

A healthcare provider is implementing a new patient data system. What should be their primary consideration to ensure compliance?

- A) Implementing safeguards that comply with the Health Insurance Portability and Accountability Act (HIPAA)
- B) Developing a comprehensive privacy policy for patient information
- C) Enhancing system security to prevent unauthorized access
- D) Conducting regular training on data protection policies

Correct Answer: A

Explanation: For healthcare providers, HIPAA compliance is essential when implementing new systems that handle patient data. This act requires the protection and confidential handling of protected health information, and compliance ensures that patient data is secure and privacy is maintained.

Question 415

An international bank is deploying a new transaction system. What is the first step they should take to ensure compliance with global financial regulations?

- A) Implementing a new user authentication system to enhance security
- B) Conducting a compliance audit to identify any regulatory misalignments
- C) Integrating advanced encryption methods for data transmission
- D) Upgrading security protocols to meet ISO/IEC 27001 standards

Correct Answer: B

Explanation: Conducting a compliance audit is the first step for any financial institution implementing new systems to ensure alignment with global financial regulations. This audit will help identify gaps in the current system alignment with regulatory requirements, enabling the institution to address these gaps effectively and maintain compliance.

Question 416

Which regulation requires US companies to protect personally identifiable information (PII)?

- A) General Data Protection Regulation (GDPR)
- B) Children's Online Privacy Protection Act (COPPA)
- C) Health Insurance Portability and Accountability Act (HIPAA)
- D) Sarbanes-Oxley Act (SOX)

Correct Answer: B

Explanation: COPPA specifically addresses the need to protect children's privacy in the digital environment, requiring companies to have clear policies regarding the collection and processing of children's data. This is especially relevant for U.S. companies that provide services directly accessible to children under the age of 13.

Question 417

In cybersecurity, what international standard provides guidelines for information security management systems (ISMS)?

- A) ISO/IEC 27001
- B) National Institute of Standards and Technology (NIST)
- C) Payment Card Industry Data Security Standard (PCI DSS)
- D) General Data Protection Regulation (GDPR)

Correct Answer: A

Explanation: ISO/IEC 27001 is an international standard that provides specifications for an information security management system (ISMS), allowing organizations to manage the security of assets such as financial information, intellectual property, employee details, and information entrusted by third parties.

Question 418

Fill in the blank: The _____ Act is a significant legal framework in the UK that governs the processing of personal data.

- A) Electronic Communications
- B) Computer Misuse
- C) Data Protection
- D) Digital Millennium Copyright

Correct Answer: C

Explanation: The Data Protection Act in the UK lays down the law on how to handle people's personal data, which is essential for any organization operating within or dealing with residents of the UK to comply with local privacy regulations.

Question 419

A tech company operates across multiple continents. To manage compliance, they need a framework for aligning with various privacy laws. What should be their first step?

- A) Implementing region-specific compliance strategies
- B) Conducting a comprehensive legal audit to identify applicable laws
- C) Reviewing and adjusting internal policies regularly
- D) Establishing a centralized legal team to handle compliance issues

Correct Answer: B

Explanation: Conducting a comprehensive legal audit is critical for a global tech company to understand the different compliance requirements across the jurisdictions in which they operate. This first step ensures that all necessary legal frameworks are considered and compliance gaps are identified.

Question 420

An e-commerce company is assessing its obligations under various national laws where it operates. What is the best initial approach to ensure legal compliance with international e-commerce transactions?

- A) Developing a compliance program based on the most stringent regulations
- B) Consulting with legal experts from each country of operation
- C) Standardizing data protection measures across all operating regions
- D) Adapting business practices to align with European Union standards

Correct Answer: A

Explanation: Developing a compliance program based on the most stringent regulations ensures that an e-commerce company can meet or exceed the requirements in all jurisdictions where it operates, thereby minimizing the risk of legal non-compliance and enhancing customer trust.

Question 421

What is the most important element to consider when developing a new security policy for data protection?

- A) Strict adherence to the least privilege principle
- B) Inclusion of all possible technological solutions
- C) Alignment with business objectives and legal requirements
- D) Focusing solely on technological defenses

Correct Answer: C

Explanation: Security policies must align with both the business objectives to support the company's mission and legal requirements to ensure compliance. This alignment helps ensure that the policies are not only enforceable but also beneficial in protecting the company's assets while adhering to regulatory standards.

Question 422

Which component should be included in every security policy to ensure it can be enforced effectively?

- A) Mandatory biannual reviews
- B) An outline of the policy development process
- C) Specific penalties for non-compliance

- D) Definitions of technical terms and jargon

Correct Answer: C

Explanation: Including specific penalties for non-compliance in a security policy ensures that the rules are taken seriously and that there are clear repercussions for failing to adhere to the policy. This helps to enforce the policy effectively across the organization.

Question 423

Fill in the blank: All security policies must be _____ to reflect current threats and technologies.

- A) continuously monitored
- B) regularly updated
- C) thoroughly documented
- D) systematically tested

Correct Answer: B

Explanation: Regular updates to security policies are crucial as they must evolve to address new threats and changes in technology. This ongoing revision process ensures that the policies remain relevant and effective in mitigating risks to the organization.

Question 424

A company is revising its security policies after a data breach. What should be their first step to ensure the policies are comprehensive?

- A) Implementing stronger password policies
- B) Upgrading cybersecurity software solutions
- C) Conducting a risk assessment to identify new vulnerabilities

- D) Reviewing the access rights of all employees

Correct Answer: C

Explanation: Conducting a risk assessment as the first step in revising security policies ensures that all changes are based on an understanding of current threats and vulnerabilities. This approach helps to prioritize areas that need attention and ensures that the policies address the most pressing security concerns.

Question 425

An organization plans to expand its operations internationally. What key factor must be considered when updating its security policies?

- A) Localizing security protocols to fit regional regulations
- B) Integrating international standards and compliance requirements
- C) Aligning with the headquarters' country legal standards
- D) Ensuring all data is encrypted, both at rest and in transit

Correct Answer: B

Explanation: When expanding operations internationally, integrating international standards and compliance requirements into security policies is essential. This ensures that the organization remains compliant across different regulatory environments, reducing legal risks and enhancing the security posture globally.

Question 426

Which risk management framework emphasizes the alignment of risk management processes with organizational governance?

- A) Project Management Body of Knowledge (PMBOK)

- B) Information Technology Infrastructure Library (ITIL)
- C) Committee of Sponsoring Organizations of the Treadway Commission (COSO) ERM
- D) ISO/IEC 27001

Correct Answer: C

Explanation: The COSO ERM framework is designed to align risk management with organizational governance, helping organizations achieve their objectives through effective risk assessment and management integrated with governance processes.

Question 427

What does the NIST Cybersecurity Framework primarily aim to provide organizations?

- A) A certification program for cybersecurity professionals
- B) A set of guidelines to improve cybersecurity and resilience
- C) A comprehensive list of IT security standards
- D) A regulatory framework for compliance with international standards

Correct Answer: B

Explanation: The NIST Cybersecurity Framework provides organizations with a structured set of guidelines designed to help improve their cybersecurity posture and resilience against cyber attacks. It is particularly noted for its flexibility and applicability to a wide range of industries.

Question 428

Fill in the blank: ISO 27005 is focused on risk management specific to _____ security.

- A) digital
- B) information

- C) network
- D) operational

Correct Answer: B

Explanation: ISO 27005 provides a focused approach on managing risks related to information security, making it an essential tool for organizations that prioritize the security of their information assets.

Question 429

A financial institution is implementing a risk management framework to address digital security threats. Which framework should they consider first for comprehensive risk analysis and mitigation strategies?

- A) National Institute of Standards and Technology (NIST)
- B) Committee of Sponsoring Organizations of the Treadway Commission (COSO) ERM
- C) Operationally Critical Threat, Asset, and Vulnerability Evaluation (OCTAVE)
- D) ISO 27005

Correct Answer: C

Explanation: OCTAVE is specifically developed to address complex and operational threats in environments like financial institutions, offering a robust methodology for identifying and mitigating risks through a comprehensive analysis of organizational vulnerabilities and security practices.

Question 430

An IT company wants to assess the potential financial impact of cyber risks. Which framework provides a quantitative approach to evaluating such risks?

- A) Cybersecurity Maturity Model Certification (CMMC)
- B) Factor Analysis of Information Risk (FAIR) RM
- C) Information Risk Management Association (IRMA)
- D) Risk Management Framework (RMF)

Correct Answer: B

Explanation: The FAIR RM framework offers a quantitative method to evaluate and analyze cybersecurity risks, focusing on the financial impact, which helps organizations make informed decisions on risk management by calculating potential loss in financial terms.

Question 431

What is the primary objective of Enterprise Risk Management (ERM)?

- A) Enhancing organizational resilience by adopting aggressive risk postures
- B) Minimizing operational losses through effective control measures
- C) Ensuring compliance with international regulatory standards
- D) Aligning risk management practices with business strategy to maximize value

Correct Answer: D

Explanation: ERM aims to align risk management with the overall business strategy to ensure that all risks are managed in a way that supports and maximizes business value. This alignment helps organizations not only mitigate risks but also capitalize on opportunities in a strategic manner.

Question 432

Which is a critical first step in integrating ERM into business processes?

- A) Integrating risk management software across all business units

- B) Identifying key risk indicators that align with business objectives
- C) Setting up a centralized risk management department
- D) Conducting annual risk reviews at the organizational level

Correct Answer: B

Explanation: Identifying key risk indicators that align with business objectives is essential for integrating ERM effectively. This allows organizations to monitor risks that are most critical to their strategic goals and ensure that risk management efforts are focused where they can have the greatest impact on business success.

Question 433

Fill in the blank: ERM frameworks typically require alignment with the organization's _____ goals.

- A) operational
- B) financial
- C) environmental
- D) strategic

Correct Answer: D

Explanation: Strategic goals are fundamental to ERM frameworks because aligning risk management with these goals ensures that the organization's risk-taking is purposeful and contributes to achieving its overarching objectives.

Question 434

A corporation is expanding into a new market sector known for regulatory complexities. What ERM strategy should they prioritize?

- A) Developing a risk-aware culture through continuous education and training
- B) Increasing investment in risk transfer strategies such as insurance
- C) Focusing on aggressive market expansion regardless of risk factors
- D) Implementing strict financial controls to manage economic exposure

Correct Answer: A

Explanation: Developing a risk-aware culture involves educating and training all levels of the organization on the importance of risk management and their role in the ERM process. This strategy is particularly important when entering markets with complex regulatory environments, as it ensures all employees understand the risks and how to manage them effectively.

Question 435

An IT firm is assessing its project portfolio for risks associated with emerging technologies. What is the most effective ERM approach for this scenario?

- A) Relying solely on technology-based solutions to mitigate risks
- B) Encouraging rapid deployment of emerging technologies to gain market advantage
- C) Delegating risk management responsibilities to technology leads
- D) Performing a comprehensive risk assessment on new technologies before adoption

Correct Answer: D

Explanation: Performing a comprehensive risk assessment on new technologies before adoption is crucial in managing risks associated with emerging technologies. This approach allows the IT firm to understand potential threats and opportunities associated with these technologies and to make informed decisions on their deployment and management.

Question 436

Which protocol ensures secure transmission of personal data in compliance with GDPR guidelines?

- A) Transmission Control Protocol (TCP) ensures data is transmitted reliably, without focusing on secure transmission of personal data.
- B) Simple Mail Transfer Protocol (SMTP) is used for sending emails and does not provide encryption or secure data transmission on its own.
- C) Hypertext Transfer Protocol Secure (HTTPS) uses SSL/TLS to secure data transmitted over the Internet, ensuring confidentiality and integrity.
- D) Secure Socket Layer (SSL) encryption is widely used to encrypt data in transit, ensuring that intercepted communications cannot be read by unauthorized parties.

Correct Answer: D

Explanation: SSL encryption is crucial for complying with GDPR's requirement to protect data during transmission, preventing unauthorized access or disclosure.

Question 437

Under GDPR, a company must report a data breach within how many hours?

- A) 72 hours is the maximum time allowed for reporting a data breach, ensuring timely notification to affected individuals and regulators.
- B) 96 hours provides a longer window that exceeds GDPR requirements and could potentially harm prompt response efforts.
- C) 48 hours provides a stricter timeframe that some organizations may voluntarily adopt, but it is not the standard requirement under GDPR.
- D) 24 hours is often considered too short to feasibly investigate and report a data breach comprehensively, not aligning with GDPR requirements.

Correct Answer: A

Explanation: GDPR mandates a maximum of 72 hours for reporting significant data breaches, aiming to ensure that all stakeholders are promptly informed and can take necessary actions to mitigate any adverse effects.

Question 438

What type of personal data does CCPA protect that GDPR does not explicitly cover?

- A) Biometric information, such as fingerprints and facial recognition data, is specifically protected under CCPA, reflecting its sensitive nature.
- B) Geolocation data, indicating an individual's physical location, is given explicit protection under CCPA, enhancing privacy protections.
- C) Internet browsing history, commonly collected for targeted advertising, is explicitly mentioned under CCPA but not under GDPR.
- D) Credit information, including credit scores and financial status, is protected under both GDPR and CCPA, but not unique to CCPA.

Correct Answer: A

Explanation: CCPA uniquely categorizes biometric information as personal information, requiring specific safeguards and consumer consent before collection, demonstrating its broader scope in protecting privacy compared to GDPR.

Question 439

Fill in the blank: In the context of GDPR, the right to be forgotten is also known as the right to _____.

- A) Consent; this term relates to obtaining permission to process personal data but does not address the removal of data.
- B) Access; this right allows individuals to see the data an organization holds about them, not involving data deletion.
- C) Rectification; this right allows individuals to have inaccurate personal data corrected, which is not specifically about deleting data.
- D) Erasure; this right allows individuals to request the deletion of their personal data under certain conditions, emphasizing data control.

Correct Answer: D

Explanation: The right to erasure, or the right to be forgotten, empowers individuals within the EU to have their personal data deleted under certain circumstances, thus promoting autonomy over one's personal information in compliance with GDPR.

Question 440

An organization based in the US collects data from EU citizens. Which regulation primarily governs the handling of this data?

- A) The Privacy Shield Framework was designed to facilitate data transfers between the EU and the US, but it focuses more on data transfer than data handling.
- B) California Consumer Privacy Act (CCPA) governs data protection for California residents, not applicable to data from EU citizens.
- C) Federal Information Security Management Act (FISMA) applies to US federal data systems and does not cover private sector organizations or EU citizen data.
- D) General Data Protection Regulation (GDPR) applies regardless of the organization's location, focusing on protecting the data of EU citizens.

Correct Answer: D

Explanation: GDPR regulates the processing of EU citizens' data by any entity worldwide, which means a US-based company must comply when dealing with EU citizens' data, ensuring the protection of their privacy rights regardless of the company's location.

Question 441

What is the primary tool used for continuous monitoring of network security compliance?

- A) Security Information and Event Management (SIEM) systems aggregate and analyze activity from many different resources across your enterprise.

- B) Anti-virus software scans and removes malicious software but does not monitor for compliance with security policies.
- C) Firewalls manage and monitor network traffic based on predetermined security rules, but they do not provide detailed compliance reports.
- D) Intrusion Detection Systems (IDS) are set to monitor network traffic and compare it against a database of known threats, which is not continuous.

Correct Answer: A

Explanation: SIEM systems are essential for continuous monitoring as they provide a comprehensive and centralized view of security events within an organization, which is crucial for meeting compliance requirements and detecting potential security breaches in real time.

Question 442

In an audit report, what is critical to include when detailing compliance with data protection regulations?

- A) A list of all employees who have completed data protection training is beneficial but not critical for showing compliance in an audit report.
- B) The company's policy on data retention should be included but is not as critical as showing how data is actively protected.
- C) Evidence of data encryption methods used to protect sensitive information should be documented to demonstrate compliance with security standards.
- D) Details of the audit method used can be included but are not as crucial as showing how data is protected according to regulations.

Correct Answer: C

Explanation: Including evidence of how data is protected, such as the encryption methods used, directly addresses regulatory requirements for data protection and is essential for demonstrating compliance in an audit report, as it shows practical steps taken to secure data.

Question 443

Fill in the blank: Auditing tools that track user activities and flag unusual access patterns are called _____.

- A) Continuous monitoring tools; while they monitor systems, they do not specifically analyze user behavior or flag anomalies.
- B) Log management tools; these are primarily used for gathering and storing log data, not specifically for monitoring unusual access patterns.
- C) Compliance tracking software; this is too broad a term and does not specifically refer to monitoring for unusual access patterns.
- D) Anomaly detection systems; these tools automatically identify deviations from normal operations, suggesting potential security violations.

Correct Answer: D

Explanation: Anomaly detection systems are specifically designed to monitor for unusual access patterns or behaviors in the network, which is vital for identifying potential security incidents early and maintaining compliance by ensuring that all user activities are within normal parameters.

Question 444

An organization implements a new compliance policy across its departments. How should the compliance be audited to ensure full adoption?

- A) Rely solely on self-reporting from department heads, which might not accurately reflect actual compliance levels.
- B) Perform a single, comprehensive audit annually, which may not identify non-compliance issues that arise mid-year in different departments.
- C) Issue an online survey to all employees to gauge their understanding of the new policies, which lacks the thoroughness of an audit.
- D) Conduct a series of department-specific audits followed by training sessions to address any discrepancies found in the initial audits.

Correct Answer: D

Explanation: Conducting department-specific audits followed by training ensures that all areas of the organization are compliant with the new policies and that any gaps in compliance are immediately addressed, which is crucial for full adoption and effective implementation of compliance policies.

Question 445

During a routine compliance check, a security officer finds unauthorized access to sensitive data. What is the first step in compliance oversight?

- A) Initiate an immediate system-wide audit, which might be premature without first understanding the specific nature of the unauthorized access.
- B) Conduct an interview with the person who accessed the data, which may not immediately address the compliance aspects of the incident.
- C) Shut down the system to prevent further unauthorized access, which could disrupt business operations unnecessarily.
- D) Report the incident to the compliance department to assess the breach and determine necessary corrective actions based on policy guidelines.

Correct Answer: D

Explanation: Reporting the incident to the compliance department first is crucial as it ensures that the breach is handled according to established compliance and regulatory procedures, prioritizing proper assessment and response to the incident according to policy guidelines.

Question 446

When establishing an incident response plan, what is the most crucial factor to consider first?

- A) Deciding on the budget for incident response tools and training
- B) Identifying the critical assets and systems that could be affected by incidents
- C) Selection of an external cybersecurity firm to assist in incident response
- D) Determining the communication strategy with external stakeholders

Correct Answer: B

Explanation: Identifying critical assets and systems first ensures that the incident response plan prioritizes actions based on potential impact, safeguarding key organizational assets effectively.

Question 447

What essential document outlines the roles and responsibilities of the incident response team?

- A) Business Continuity Plan
- B) Service Level Agreement
- C) Standard Operating Procedures document
- D) Incident Response Policy

Correct Answer: D

Explanation: The Incident Response Policy is foundational as it establishes clear guidelines and authority, enabling a swift and structured response to incidents.

Question 448

Fill in the blank: ___ is the step in the incident response plan that focuses on minimizing the impact of the security incident.

- A) Containment
- B) Recovery
- C) Lessons Learned
- D) Eradication

Correct Answer: A

Explanation: Containment aims to limit the spread and escalation of an incident, reducing damage and maintaining business operations, which is crucial before moving to eradication and recovery.

Question 449

A company is hit by a ransomware attack; what should their incident response team's first step be according to the plan?

- A) Convene the incident response team to assess the situation and execute the initial response
- B) Notify all company employees and instruct them to change passwords
- C) Isolate the affected network segments to prevent further spread
- D) Contact law enforcement and external cybersecurity help

Correct Answer: A

Explanation: Convening the incident response team is essential to assess the situation comprehensively and determine the necessary steps to mitigate the attack efficiently.

Question 450

During a network breach, what type of analysis is critical for understanding the nature of the attack?

- A) Forensic analysis to collect and examine evidence from affected systems
- B) Threat intelligence to predict potential future attack vectors
- C) Log analysis to detect the breach time and possibly involved accounts
- D) Behavioral analysis to determine the motive and method of the attackers

Correct Answer: A

Explanation: Forensic analysis is critical for understanding how the breach occurred, preserving evidence, and preventing future incidents by identifying the source and method of the attack.

Question 451

Which type of control is primarily used to prevent unauthorized physical access to network resources?

- A) Security guard patrols
- B) Biometric access systems
- C) Card key access systems
- D) Mantrap entry systems

Correct Answer: B

Explanation: Biometric access systems provide a high level of security by using unique physical characteristics of individuals (like fingerprints or retina patterns), which are hard to replicate, thus effectively preventing unauthorized access.

Question 452

What type of security control involves analyzing network traffic to detect patterns indicative of a cyber attack?

- A) Intrusion detection systems (IDS)
- B) Firewall monitoring tools
- C) Antivirus software
- D) Encryption tools

Correct Answer: A

Explanation: Intrusion detection systems are critical in the security infrastructure as they monitor network traffic for suspicious activity and known attack patterns, allowing organizations to detect potential threats early.

Question 453

Fill in the blank: ___ controls are designed to correct systems or processes post-incident to restore functionality and security.

- A) Detective
- B) Compensatory
- C) Preventive
- D) Corrective

Correct Answer: D

Explanation: Corrective controls are implemented after a security breach or failure has been detected to repair and restore system operations, ensuring that the affected systems are brought back to their proper functioning state.

Question 454

In a scenario where an organization detects an unauthorized entry into their network, what type of control helps in identifying the breach source?

- A) Real-time threat intelligence
- B) Network segmentation
- C) Incident simulation testing
- D) Log analysis

Correct Answer: D

Explanation: Log analysis is an effective detective control as it involves the examination of system logs to trace the source of a security breach, helping to understand how the breach occurred and how similar incidents can be prevented.

Question 455

When configuring a firewall to restrict unauthorized access, which type of security control is being implemented?

- A) Detective controls
- B) Preventive controls
- C) Corrective controls
- D) Recovery controls

Correct Answer: B

Explanation: Implementing firewall rules that specifically block or restrict access based on pre-defined security policies acts as a preventive measure, aiming to stop security threats before they can impact the network.

Question 456

Which control framework focuses on aligning IT goals with business objectives while managing IT risks effectively?

- A) TOGAF
- B) COBIT
- C) ISO 27001
- D) ITIL

Correct Answer: B

Explanation: COBIT is designed to bridge the gap between business requirements and IT, offering a governance framework that ensures IT operations support business goals while mitigating IT-related risks.

Question 457

Which control framework provides a detailed set of security and privacy controls for federal information systems?

- A) NIST SP 800-53
- B) HIPAA
- C) PCI DSS
- D) ISO 27001

Correct Answer: A

Explanation: NIST SP 800-53 provides a comprehensive catalog of security and privacy controls specifically tailored for federal information systems and organizations, addressing a wide range of IT security issues.

Question 458

Fill in the blank: ___ is a control framework that emphasizes internal controls and is widely used for corporate governance.

- A) COBIT
- B) COSO
- C) NIST SP 800-53
- D) ISO 31000

Correct Answer: B

Explanation: COSO emphasizes internal controls and governance, helping organizations manage operational, compliance, and reporting risks. It is commonly used to enhance corporate governance.

Question 459

A company is implementing a new risk management process and wants to ensure that IT supports business strategies while managing risks. Which framework would best guide their efforts?

- A) FAIR
- B) ISO 31000
- C) COBIT
- D) COSO

Correct Answer: C

Explanation: COBIT is a widely recognized framework that provides guidance on how IT should be governed and managed in alignment with business goals while effectively managing risks.

Question 460

In a scenario where an organization needs to assess its overall security posture across all departments, which control framework offers the most comprehensive set of controls for evaluating IT and cybersecurity risks?

- A) COBIT
- B) ISO 27001
- C) NIST SP 800-53
- D) COSO

Correct Answer: C

Explanation: NIST SP 800-53 is an in-depth framework offering a large number of controls for evaluating and improving an organization's security and privacy posture across various domains.

Question 461

What is the most important step in preparing for an internal IT security audit?

- A) Gathering evidence of past incidents and security breaches
- B) Collecting detailed data logs from all IT systems
- C) Selecting the right team of external consultants to oversee the process
- D) Defining the scope and objectives of the audit with the audit team

Correct Answer: D

Explanation: Defining the scope and objectives ensures that the audit covers all relevant areas of IT security, aligning the audit with business goals and potential risk areas, making the audit more focused and effective.

Question 462

Which aspect of an external audit is crucial for ensuring transparency between the auditor and the organization?

- A) Negotiating the terms of the audit with external auditors
- B) Hiring an external auditing firm specializing in cybersecurity
- C) Ensuring auditors have access to all company systems
- D) Clear communication and proper documentation of audit findings

Correct Answer: D

Explanation: Clear communication and documentation between the auditor and the organization are essential for transparency. This helps both parties understand the findings and agree on any recommendations, ensuring there is no confusion during the audit process.

Question 463

Fill in the blank: During the planning phase of an internal audit, __ is conducted to identify potential risks and the scope of the audit.

- A) A risk assessment
- B) A business continuity plan
- C) A compliance checklist
- D) An incident response plan

Correct Answer: A

Explanation: A risk assessment during the planning phase identifies areas of potential concern and prioritizes them for the audit. This allows the audit team to focus on the most critical areas and ensures a thorough evaluation.

Question 464

A company is preparing for an external IT audit to comply with regulatory requirements. What is the first action the organization should take to ensure successful audit results?

- A) Restrict employee access to sensitive systems and information
- B) Create an internal review team to conduct a pre-audit
- C) Prepare audit reports to share with stakeholders
- D) Review the company's IT security policies and ensure they are up to date

Correct Answer: D

Explanation: Reviewing and updating the IT security policies is the first step before an external audit. This helps to align the organization's security practices with current regulatory standards, increasing the chances of a successful audit.

Question 465

In a scenario where an internal audit reveals significant security gaps, what should be the immediate focus of the audit team's next steps?

- A) Implement corrective actions to address the security gaps
- B) Monitor security alerts in real-time during the auditing process
- C) Assign roles and responsibilities to the IT department for remediation
- D) Document all findings and monitor remediation progress closely

Correct Answer: A

Explanation: Implementing corrective actions immediately is the best course of action when security gaps are discovered. This helps prevent further vulnerabilities from being exploited and strengthens the organization's overall security posture before the next audit stage.

Question 466

What is the most effective metric for tracking the time it takes to respond to a security incident?

- A) Incident resolution time
- B) Mean time to respond (MTTR)
- C) Incident severity score
- D) Time to contain threats

Correct Answer: B

Explanation: Mean time to respond (MTTR) is a key performance indicator for measuring how quickly the security team can react to and mitigate security incidents, helping organizations reduce downtime and damage.

Question 467

Which metric is essential for evaluating how well security controls prevent unauthorized access attempts?

- A) Success rate of access control mechanisms
- B) Failed login attempts per month
- C) Intrusion detection rate
- D) Firewall block rate

Correct Answer: C

Explanation: The intrusion detection rate tracks how effectively a system identifies and responds to unauthorized access attempts, ensuring that controls in place are working as expected and reducing the risk of breaches.

Question 468

Fill in the blank: ___ is the metric used to measure the total number of security vulnerabilities detected in a given period.

- A) Employee security awareness score
- B) Patch management efficiency
- C) Vulnerability detection rate
- D) Encryption compliance rate

Correct Answer: C

Explanation: The vulnerability detection rate measures the total number of vulnerabilities found in systems over time. By tracking this, organizations can gauge their ability to detect and address security weaknesses proactively.

Question 469

A company wants to track how frequently its systems are targeted by malware. Which metric should they use to monitor this trend?

- A) System patch cycle time
- B) Number of detected phishing emails
- C) Intrusion attempts per day
- D) Malware detection frequency

Correct Answer: D

Explanation: Malware detection frequency is the metric that tracks how often malware is identified within the organization's systems, helping the security team monitor and understand the patterns of malware targeting the infrastructure.

Question 470

In a scenario where an organization is trying to improve its incident detection capabilities, which metric should be prioritized to measure the success of this initiative?

- A) Time to detect incidents
- B) Security monitoring effectiveness
- C) Incident response success rate
- D) Number of audit failures identified

Correct Answer: A

Explanation: Time to detect incidents measures how quickly an organization can identify an ongoing security breach, ensuring that the organization improves its detection capabilities and reduces the dwell time of potential attackers.

Question 471

What approach allows a security analyst to determine the economic impact of a potential breach by assessing asset value and potential loss magnitude?

- A) Automated risk assessment tools, which use software to predict and quantify risk exposures.
- B) Quantitative risk analysis, which relies on precise numeric values to estimate potential impacts.
- C) Risk mapping, which visually outlines risks and their relationships to business processes.
- D) Qualitative risk assessment approach, which considers asset categorization and subjective estimates of impact.

Correct Answer: D

Explanation: The qualitative risk assessment approach is highlighted as it focuses on categorizing assets and using subjective estimates rather than specific numerical data. This method helps in scenarios where precise data may not be available, allowing for a broad analysis of potential impacts based on perceived threat levels and vulnerabilities.

Question 472

During a risk assessment, a cybersecurity manager uses a specific model to predict the probable financial loss from attacks. Which model is typically used?

- A) Annual Loss Expectancy (ALE) model, which combines annual rate of occurrence with single loss expectancy.
- B) Value at Risk (VaR) model, which measures the risk of loss on investments.
- C) Risk matrix approach, which categorizes risks based on their severity and likelihood.
- D) Threat assessment model, which focuses on identifying vulnerabilities and the likelihood of their exploitation.

Correct Answer: A

Explanation: The Annual Loss Expectancy (ALE) model is ideal for predicting financial loss as it combines the likelihood of an event occurring within a year with the expected cost of losses from such an event. This model provides a clear, quantifiable measure that aids organizations in financial planning and risk prioritization.

Question 473

Fill in the blank: The technique that applies statistical methods to model risk events and their financial impacts is known as _____.

- A) Predictive analysis, which uses historical data to predict future risks.
- B) Monte Carlo simulation, which provides a detailed range of possible outcomes and their probabilities.
- C) Delphi method, a structured communication technique using a panel of experts.
- D) Fault tree analysis, a deductive reasoning method to analyze underlying causes of risks.

Correct Answer: B

Explanation: Monte Carlo simulation is used in risk quantification due to its ability to model different outcomes based on varying risk variables, providing a probabilistic range of potential losses. This method is especially useful in complex environments where multiple risk factors interact in unpredictable ways.

Question 474

An IT company assesses risks by simulating attacks and recording potential losses over time to determine the most damaging scenarios. What is this method called?

- A) Threat modeling, which identifies security threats and rates them based on risk.
- B) Annual risk assessment, a yearly review of identified risks and their potential impacts.
- C) Risk simulation, a process that includes a wide range of attack scenarios and potential impacts.
- D) Qualitative risk assessment, which uses subjective methods to determine potential impacts.

Correct Answer: C

Explanation: Risk simulation involves creating simulations of attacks to observe potential losses, which helps in understanding the most harmful threats and preparing more effectively. This method provides dynamic insights into risk management by accounting for a variety of attack vectors and their possible consequences.

Question 475

A security professional is estimating the potential losses from security breaches over a projected period. They consider various factors like recovery costs and business interruption. What method are they using?

- A) Business impact analysis, which focuses primarily on recovery time and critical system priorities.
- B) Delphi method, involving expert opinions to forecast potential losses in the future.
- C) Quantitative risk analysis, which uses numeric values to estimate risk levels and

potential impacts.
- D) Risk registry, a document that lists all identified risks and their mitigation strategies.

Correct Answer: C

Explanation: Quantitative risk analysis is crucial for calculating potential financial impacts by applying numeric values to risk components such as the likelihood of risk occurrence and its potential impact. This approach aids in making informed decisions by quantifying the severity of risks and their potential financial implications.

Question 476

What is the primary purpose of conducting a Business Impact Analysis (BIA) in cybersecurity?

- A) To technically evaluate the performance of installed security measures and their efficiency.
- B) To determine the most cost-effective security investment by analyzing past incidents.
- C) To comply with industry regulations that mandate regular security assessments and reports.
- D) To identify critical business processes and the impact of disruptions to these processes due to security incidents.

Correct Answer: D

Explanation: Conducting a Business Impact Analysis (BIA) is critical for identifying essential business functions and evaluating the potential consequences of disruptions caused by security incidents. This analysis helps prioritize recovery strategies and resource allocation to ensure business continuity.

Question 477

During a BIA, what key factor must be evaluated to determine the severity of a security incident's impact on business operations?

- A) Business Impact Score, which ranks the effects of incidents on various business metrics.
- B) Impact probability, which assesses the likelihood of different types of security breaches.
- C) Recovery Time Objective (RTO), which defines the maximum acceptable downtime for business processes.
- D) Residual Risk Level, which measures the risk remaining after security controls are applied.

Correct Answer: C

Explanation: The Recovery Time Objective (RTO) is vital in a BIA because it defines the maximum amount of time that business processes can be down after a disruption before causing significant harm to the organization. Understanding RTO helps in planning effective recovery strategies to restore services within an acceptable timeframe.

Question 478

Fill in the blank: In Business Impact Analysis, the estimated time by which a business process must be restored to avoid unacceptable consequences is called the _____.

- A) Business Continuity Plan (BCP).
- B) Recovery Time Objective (RTO).
- C) Maximum Tolerable Downtime (MTD).
- D) Disaster Recovery Time (DRT).

Correct Answer: B

Explanation: The Recovery Time Objective (RTO) is a key concept in Business Impact Analysis as it sets the target time for recovering critical processes to prevent unacceptable consequences related to a disruption. Accurately setting the RTO is crucial for maintaining operational continuity during and after a security incident.

Question 479

A company is assessing the impact of data breaches on their online service. They analyze how long they can operate without this service before significant damage occurs. What BIA element are they focusing on?

- A) Business Continuity Plan (BCP) requirements, ensuring all regulatory needs are met.
- B) Recovery Time Objective (RTO), focusing on the maximum tolerable period of disruption.
- C) Recovery Point Objective (RPO), focusing on data loss and recovery accuracy.
- D) Service Level Agreement (SLA) terms, reviewing penalties for downtime breaches.

Correct Answer: B

Explanation: Focusing on the Recovery Time Objective (RTO) during a BIA allows a company to assess the maximum acceptable outage time. This focus helps in strategizing how to maintain operations or quickly restore them to mitigate severe service and financial impacts during disruptions.

Question 480

When performing a BIA, which metric would be crucial to assess financial losses due to a prolonged system downtime following a cyber attack?

- A) Operational disruption metrics, focusing on workflow interruptions and employee productivity.
- B) Reputational damage assessment, evaluating long-term impacts on brand and customer loyalty.
- C) Indirect financial losses, including lost customer trust and potential legal ramifications.
- D) Direct financial losses, calculating the immediate cost implications of system unavailability.

Correct Answer: D

Explanation: Direct financial losses are a crucial metric in a BIA when assessing the impact of system downtime. This measurement helps in understanding the immediate financial consequences of operational halts, guiding the prioritization of recovery efforts and investments in resilience to mitigate such risks effectively.

Question 481

What is the main goal of security awareness training in a corporate environment?

- A) To prepare the IT staff exclusively for the management of cybersecurity infrastructure.
- B) To assess the technical skills of new employees in handling the organization's security systems.
- C) To equip employees with the knowledge and skills needed to recognize and prevent security threats.
- D) To fulfill legal requirements that mandate regular training on workplace safety and security.

Correct Answer: C

Explanation: Security awareness training is essential for empowering all employees to act as the first line of defense against security threats. By equipping them with the necessary knowledge and skills, they can recognize potential threats and respond appropriately, thereby reducing the risk to the organization.

Question 482

A security manager is planning to update the training modules after a phishing attack. What should be the primary focus of the new training content?

- A) Focusing on improving the physical security measures at the workplace.
- B) Educating employees on the indicators of phishing and the best practices for responding to suspicious emails.

- C) Implementing stricter access controls to reduce the risk of unauthorized access.
- D) Increasing the complexity of security passwords and protocols used by the company.

Correct Answer: B

Explanation: Following a phishing attack, it is crucial to focus on educating employees about recognizing phishing attempts and understanding the correct actions to take when they encounter suspicious emails. This specific focus helps mitigate one of the most common and effective types of cyber threats.

Question 483

Fill in the blank: Regular updates to security awareness training ensure that employees are informed about the latest _____ threats.

- A) software updates.
- B) cyber security.
- C) compliance standards.
- D) operational procedures.

Correct Answer: B

Explanation: Regular updates to security awareness training are vital for keeping employees informed about the latest cyber security threats. As cyber threats evolve, keeping the workforce educated on recent threats and how to combat them is critical for maintaining organizational security.

Question 484

In a multinational corporation, the security team conducts annual security awareness sessions. How should these sessions be tailored to be most effective?

- A) One-size-fits-all training modules that apply universally, regardless of regional differences.
- B) Conducted only in English to maintain consistency in training delivery across all regions.
- C) Delivered in a single, centralized location to reduce costs and ensure uniformity.
- D) Customized according to the specific security risks and cultural aspects of each country's operations.

Correct Answer: D

Explanation: Tailoring security awareness sessions according to the specific risks and cultural contexts of each country where the corporation operates enhances the relevance and effectiveness of the training. This approach ensures that the training is applicable and engaging for employees in different regions, thereby improving its overall impact.

Question 485

During a routine security audit, it was noted that employees lacked understanding of social engineering tactics. What kind of training program should be introduced?

- A) A comprehensive training module that covers various types of social engineering attacks, with practical examples and prevention strategies.
- B) Periodic quizzes and tests to assess employees' understanding of existing security policies.
- C) An annual seminar discussing general IT security trends without specific focus on social engineering.
- D) Advanced technical training on the latest encryption technologies to improve data security.

Correct Answer: A

Explanation: Introducing a comprehensive training module focused on social engineering attacks is essential when employees show a lack of understanding in this area. Such training should include practical examples and prevention strategies to help employees recognize and respond to these types of attacks effectively.

Question 486
What is a critical first step in third-party risk management?

- A) Conducting a thorough risk assessment of the vendor to evaluate their security measures.
- B) Setting up a dedicated team to interact directly with the third-party vendors.
- C) Developing an internal policy for managing all third-party interactions.
- D) Signing a non-disclosure agreement to protect any sensitive information shared.

Correct Answer: A

Explanation: Conducting a thorough risk assessment of the vendor is fundamental in third-party risk management as it helps identify and evaluate potential security risks associated with the vendor's services or products. This initial step is crucial to determine whether the vendor's security measures meet the organization's requirements and to guide subsequent risk management actions.

Question 487
When reviewing a vendor's compliance, what specific documentation should be prioritized?

- A) The vendor's latest security audit report to assess their compliance with relevant standards.
- B) Reviewing the vendor's corporate social responsibility policy for ethical practices.
- C) Checking the financial stability reports of the vendor to ensure long-term viability.
- D) Examining the vendor's environmental impact reports to evaluate sustainability.

Correct Answer: A

Explanation: Prioritizing the vendor's latest security audit report is essential when reviewing compliance because it provides a detailed and formal assessment of the vendor's adherence to security standards. This documentation is crucial for understanding the vendor's security posture and any areas of non-compliance that might affect the organization.

Question 488

Fill in the blank: Effective third-party risk management often requires implementing _____ to monitor ongoing compliance.

- A) random checks.
- B) manual inspections.
- C) periodic reviews.
- D) continuous audits.

Correct Answer: D

Explanation: Implementing continuous audits in third-party risk management allows for ongoing monitoring and ensures that the vendor consistently adheres to compliance standards. This proactive approach helps in identifying and mitigating risks arising from changes in the vendor's operations or security practices.

Question 489

A company plans to hire a cloud service provider. What is an essential action before finalizing the contract?

- A) Asking for references from other clients to confirm the provider's reliability.
- B) Conduct a detailed security assessment of the provider to ensure their practices align with company standards.
- C) Negotiating lower prices to include costs for potential security enhancements.
- D) Review the public customer feedback about the provider's services on various platforms.

Correct Answer: B

Explanation: Conducting a detailed security assessment of the cloud service provider before finalizing the contract ensures that their security practices align with the company's standards. This step is crucial to prevent security breaches and data loss, and to maintain trust and integrity in the services provided.

Question 490

An organization notices that a supplier's software has potential security vulnerabilities. What is the immediate step they should take according to third-party risk management principles?

- A) Conduct an internal audit to determine if the vulnerabilities have been exploited.
- B) Terminate the contract immediately to avoid further risk exposure.
- C) Isolate the affected systems until the supplier resolves the security issues.
- D) Request an immediate security update from the supplier to address the vulnerabilities.

Correct Answer: D

Explanation: Requesting an immediate security update from the supplier upon identifying potential security vulnerabilities aligns with best practices in third-party risk management. This immediate action helps mitigate risks by ensuring that the vulnerabilities are addressed promptly, thus maintaining the security of the organization's systems and data.

Question 491

What is the primary goal of penetration testing in the context of cybersecurity risk management?

- A) To demonstrate the effectiveness of existing security measures and tools.
- B) To comply with international cybersecurity regulations and standards.
- C) To train the IT staff on the latest cybersecurity defense techniques.

- D) To identify and exploit vulnerabilities in systems to assess the potential for unauthorized access or other malicious activity.

Correct Answer: D

Explanation: The primary goal of penetration testing is to actively exploit vulnerabilities in a system to determine the potential for unauthorized access or other forms of malicious activity. This method helps organizations understand their weaknesses and the potential impact of an attack, guiding effective security improvements.

Question 492

When conducting a vulnerability assessment, what is essential to prioritize to ensure comprehensive coverage?

- A) Newly installed network infrastructure to ensure they are integrated securely.
- B) Critical systems that store or process sensitive or proprietary information.
- C) Publicly accessible web applications to minimize public exposure.
- D) Peripheral devices such as printers and scanners that are often overlooked.

Correct Answer: B

Explanation: Prioritizing critical systems that handle sensitive or proprietary information during a vulnerability assessment is crucial because these systems, if compromised, could lead to significant financial or reputational damage. Ensuring these systems are secure helps protect the most valuable assets of the organization.

Question 493

Fill in the blank: The methodology that focuses on simulating an attacker's actions to test system defenses is called _____.

- A) risk mapping.
- B) ethical hacking.
- C) vulnerability indexing.
- D) penetration matrix.

Correct Answer: B

Explanation: Ethical hacking is a methodology where security experts simulate the actions of an attacker. This practice helps identify security weaknesses that could be exploited and allows for the development of defenses against such attacks, making it an essential part of a proactive security strategy.

Question 494

A financial institution conducts a penetration test to find potential exploits in its online banking system. What should be the main focus of this test?

- A) Checking the compliance of the system with global financial security regulations.
- B) Testing the physical security measures at bank branches to prevent onsite breaches.
- C) Identifying vulnerabilities that could be exploited to gain unauthorized access to financial data.
- D) Evaluating the user interface for ease of use and accessibility for all customers.

Correct Answer: C

Explanation: For a financial institution, the main focus of a penetration test on its online banking system should be identifying vulnerabilities that could be exploited to gain unauthorized access to financial data. This focus ensures that the most critical assets are protected and helps maintain customer trust and regulatory compliance.

Question 495

After discovering vulnerabilities in a new software release, what should a company's next step be to ensure these are addressed effectively?

- A) Schedule a future update to include fixes for the vulnerabilities.
- B) Inform all customers about the vulnerabilities to maintain transparency.
- C) Conduct an internal audit to review the development processes.
- D) Prioritize the vulnerabilities based on risk and begin immediate remediation.

Correct Answer: D

Explanation: After identifying vulnerabilities in new software, the immediate next step is to prioritize these vulnerabilities based on their risk level and initiate remediation processes. This approach helps in managing the most critical vulnerabilities first and reduces the window of opportunity for attackers to exploit these weaknesses.

Question 496

What is the primary purpose of security dashboards in cybersecurity monitoring?

- A) To document every security incident within the organization for compliance purposes.
- B) To automate the response to all security incidents detected by the system.
- C) To provide a centralized visual representation of critical security alerts and the current threat landscape.
- D) To replace the need for manual security checks and reporting within the IT department.

Correct Answer: C

Explanation: Security dashboards serve primarily to provide a centralized, visual representation of key security alerts and the overall threat environment, enabling quick understanding and response to emerging threats. This centralization helps security teams monitor and manage security effectively by highlighting critical issues that need immediate attention.

Question 497

Which metric is crucial for inclusion on a security dashboard to monitor real-time threats?

- A) Frequency of system backups as a measure of data protection effectiveness.
- B) Number of attempted security breaches in real time.
- C) Average time taken to detect a security incident from its occurrence.
- D) Total number of past resolved incidents to evaluate the security team's performance.

Correct Answer: B

Explanation: Including the number of attempted security breaches in real time on a dashboard is crucial as it allows security teams to detect and respond to threats as they occur. Real-time data ensures that the security stance is up-to-date, reflecting the most current threats and enabling immediate action to mitigate risks.

Question 498

Fill in the blank: Dashboards in cybersecurity should dynamically display _____ to facilitate quick incident response.

- A) compliance statuses.
- B) threat levels.
- C) software updates.
- D) historical trends.

Correct Answer: B

Explanation: Dynamically displaying threat levels on cybersecurity dashboards is essential because it allows security teams to quickly assess and respond to the most critical issues. This real-time information aids in prioritizing responses and allocating resources more effectively to areas of greatest need.

Question 499

A company implements a new security dashboard to track incidents across its global network. What feature should be prioritized to enhance its effectiveness?

- A) The capability to customize views according to different user roles within the organization.
- B) Real-time alerts for any changes to critical network infrastructure settings.
- C) A live feed of all network traffic to detect unauthorized access attempts.
- D) Integration with all third-party security tools currently in use by the company.

Correct Answer: A

Explanation: Customizing dashboard views according to different user roles within the organization is an important feature because it ensures that each team member accesses relevant information necessary for their specific duties. This customization enhances the effectiveness of the dashboard by ensuring that all users have the most pertinent information to their roles, improving both awareness and response times.

Question 500

During an executive meeting, a CISO uses a dashboard to report on the organization's security posture. What should the dashboard primarily display to assist in decision-making?

- A) Upcoming security maintenance and scheduled downtime of critical systems.
- B) Key security metrics like current threat levels, incident types, and resolution statuses.
- C) Detailed logs of all user activities and changes within the IT infrastructure.
- D) Financial implications of security breaches including potential and actual losses.

Correct Answer: B

Explanation: A dashboard used in executive meetings should primarily display key security metrics such as current threat levels, types of incidents, and resolution statuses. This information provides executives with a clear overview of the security posture and the effectiveness of ongoing security measures, assisting them in making informed decisions about resource allocation and policy adjustments.

www.ingramcontent.com/pod-product-compliance
Lightning Source LLC
LaVergne TN
LVHW051436050326
832903LV00030BD/3122